CONCORDE AND DISSENT

Concorde and dissent

Explaining high technology project
failures in Britain and France

ELLIOT J. FELDMAN
Harvard University

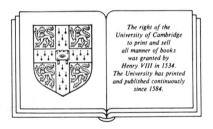

The right of the
University of Cambridge
to print and sell
all manner of books
was granted by
Henry VIII in 1534.
The University has printed
and published continuously
since 1584.

CAMBRIDGE UNIVERSITY PRESS

Cambridge

London   New York   New Rochelle

Melbourne   Sydney

Published by the Press Syndicate of the University of Cambridge
The Pitt Building, Trumpington Street, Cambridge CB2 1RP
32 East 57th Street, New York, NY 10022, USA
10 Stamford Road, Oakleigh, Melbourne 3166, Australia

First published 1985

Printed in the United States of America

Library of Congress Cataloging in Publication Data
Feldman, Elliot J.
Concorde and dissent.
1. Aeronautics and state – Great Britain – Case studies.
2. Aeronautics and state – France – Case studies.   I. Title.
HE9843.A4F45   1985   387.7′068   84–28531
ISBN 0 521 30519 5

Written under the auspices of the Center for International
Affairs, Harvard University

FOR LILY,
    who expedited completion,
AND SHIRA,
    who introduced wondrous delay

Contents

Tables, figures, and maps

x   *Tables, figures, and maps*

Preface

This book is about Concorde, a cooperative Anglo-French venture in high technology that began in 1960, and the efforts to build new international airports for London and Paris beginning in the late 1950s. The three detailed case studies have been chosen deliberately for the systematic analysis of public policy decision making in Britain and France. The overall objective is to explain why, popular images notwithstanding, neither Britain nor France has been particularly successful in the development and promotion of high technology, especially in civil aviation. The explanations, in turn, invite a reassessment of conventional comparisons in the study of Western European political systems.

Two separate methodological traditions are deployed here – the case method and comparison – with the goal of combining the virtues of each. Case studies encourage attention to detail, recognizing the significance of a good story told well; comparisons imply standards for measurement and provide the basis for judgment that is absent in the assessment of a single experience.

These cases are not "representative" of the two political systems in the sense of being typical. Typical examples would be ordinary, and these stories undoubtedly are extraordinary. That distinction, however, is what makes them "crucial" in Harry Eckstein's sense.[1] They were accorded top priority by political leaders. Exceptional resources and energy were devoted in both Britain and France to their successful accomplishment. British and French leaders did their best to reach narrowly defined goals efficiently, swiftly, and effectively. They spared no expense to coordinate intragovernmental interests and to assure coherence in policy. These cases of high-profile high technology tested the British and French systems at peak performance. The coordination, efficiency, speed, and level of achievement were to be the best the systems could produce. Less might be expected of less important government projects.

Because performance in these cases was a measure of the best the systems could produce, these cases are "crucial" bases for generalizing about Britain and France. The explanations offered for differences in these crucial cases may be applied to other examples, at least within the same category of high-profile high technology, but perhaps also in other categories of state enterprise. Criticism of system performance at its best surely must be applicable to system performance in less advantageous circumstances.

The case of Britain's attempt to build a third international airport for London is compared to the case of France's construction of Charles de Gaulle Airport outside Paris because superficially the outcomes of these like cases confirm stereotypes about British and French political systems. These most-similar experiences with different outcomes reveal on close inspection that the systems so typically contrasted bear fundamental similarities. The British and French approaches to Concorde are compared because, as a common project, there can be no doubt about equivalence in validating the comparison. Hence the cases have particular theoretical value.

These three cases also have intrinsic value, manifest in the substantial literature devoted simply to reporting about them. This literature, unfortunately, is infused with many hidden agenda of protagonists. Consequently there is one additional objective to the presentation of the cases here, to permit them to stand on their own as historically reliable documents. These cases are significant for the study of decision making and technological development, for national independence and international cooperation.

The research for this book was completed in 1980 and the writing largely in 1981. During the subsequent period of refinement and publishing there have been notable developments concerning the three cases, although none that alters the book's argument. Those developments occurring into 1982 have been integrated into the text; still others are mentioned in an epilogue.

E.J.F.

Acknowledgments

The idea for this book originated in discussions at Harvard University's Center for International Affairs as an outgrowth of a multinational study on airport development controversies. An important justification offered by decision makers for the expansion of the Paris airport system was the technological requirement of Concorde, and I was learning a great deal about the plane. Peter Jacobsohn, former editor of publications at the center, and Sidney Verba and Raymond Vernon of the center faculty, encouraged me to pursue that inquiry, especially with a focus on the transnational dimensions. I began to wonder how Britain and France, two countries long considered opposites in culture and politics and antagonists in world affairs, could overcome dissension and disagreement enough to build together the most sophisticated commercial aircraft in history – at the very time the world's technological giants, the United States and the Soviet Union, were failing.

Numerous people in Britain, France, and the United States helped me answer the questions raised by contrasts in achievement in the building of new airports and by comparisons in the approaches to Concorde. Top executives testified for me from British Airways, Air France, British Caledonian, Air Inter, Union de Transports Aériens, and Pan American World Airways; Aéroport de Paris and the British Airports Authority; Aérospatiale and Société nationale d'Etudes et Construction de Moteurs Aviation. Senior officials of the French president's cabinet, the Ministry of Transport and Civil Aviation, the Service des Bases Aériennes, and authorities in the Société Nationale des Chemins de Fer, the Régie Autonome des Transports Parisiens, the Organisme Régional d'Etudes pour l'Aménagement de la Picardie, the Institut d'Aménagement et d'Urbanisme de la Région Parisienne, and the District of Paris all provided particularly generous help with first-hand knowledge and documents. Three former French ministers of transport granted lengthy interviews.

In Britain I received extensive testimony from former members of Parliament, two former aviation ministers, and two former presidents of the Board of Trade. Senior officials in the Civil Aviation Authority, the Foreign and Commonwealth Office, the Departments of Trade and Industry, and the Department of Environment all provided extensive interviews, as did several members of the research team of the Roskill Commission.

Leading opponents of airport development in both countries, including local mayors and public officials, provided critical assessments of central government positions. Holden Withington of the Boeing Commercial Aircraft Company helped me orient the analysis of Concorde in reference to the American SST, and Chauncy Ollinger of the Friends of the Earth kept me mindful of the opposing view. The interviews in all three countries, of public officials, corporate leaders, and engaged citizens, and the special documentation discreetly made available by unusually cooperative witnesses, constitute the invaluable data essential to this study. To protect the confidentiality of some, I have chosen to neglect naming the many respondents, but they have my lasting gratitude.

I accumulated numerous personal debts as an American investigating controversial policy issues in other countries, and I especially want to thank, in Paris, Sabine Arrighi, Jean-Louis and Angèline Bourlanges, Jean-Yves Delhaye,

xvi   *Acknowledgments*

Robert Espérou, Jean-Paul Bailly, and Sylvia Duchacek for hospitality, warm friendship, wise counsel, secretarial support, and often remarkable connections. In London I owe similar debts to Don Easton, Jean and Tom Gardner, Elizabeth Johnson, Richard Simon, Scott Russell, Alison Brimelow, Phoebe Lambert, and Frank Thompson.

Elda Stifani, Lynne Bantle, Paul Rulison, and Mario Ristoratore proved exceptionally capable research assistants at different stages of this project. They each know how much their help has been appreciated.

This study cost money. The Penrose Fund of the American Philosophical Society provided a modest but timely travel grant, and the German Marshall Fund of the United States gave me a fellowship that made possible a second and essential round of data collection in Europe. Brandeis University paid for a visit to New York during the Concorde hearings, and the Center for International Affairs (particularly its Director, Samuel P. Huntington) and the University Consortium for Research on North America provided me various services and an ideal research environment.

Earlier versions of two chapters of this book were presented to the French Politics Group of the Annual Conference of Europeanists and the British Politics Group of the American Political Science Association. I am grateful especially to Jürgen Rasmussen and Ezra Suleiman for these opportunities to expose ideas and receive useful criticism. The University of Massachusetts at Amherst, through Paul Mankin and the European Studies Program there, invited me to present the overall thesis of the book, a visit that was particularly fruitful.

The entire manuscript was read and well criticized by Seyom Brown, Robert Espérou, Elizabeth Johnson, Robert Keohane, Theodore J. Lowi, Jerome Milch, Richard Simon, Gordon W. Stead, Ezra Suleiman, Frank Thompson, and several anonymous readers. Helpful comments on portions came from Jesse Pitts. All will observe significant changes resulting from their careful readings, and I am indebted to them. Sue Allen-Mills and Janis Bolster of Cambridge University Press offered enthusiastic support and wise counsel, and Christopher Leman was especially helpful for the discussion of comparative cases in the appendix. Lily Gardner Feldman diligently created the index. I should add, however, that the traditional disclaimer may require emphasis: There is enough controversy here to guarantee that those who have contributed to the final product do not necessarily agree with it. They have saved me from many errors of fact, and they have done their best to dissuade me from what some may still see as errors of interpretation.

Finishing this book entailed unexpected but joyful delays, for on many days Shira demanded and got most of my attention. Lily Gardner Feldman did all she could to enable me to finish, and I am grateful to both these women in my life for making the writing of the book more fun than I had any right to expect.

1

Compare or contrast? Britain, France, and civil aviation

Observers of Western Europe often like to compare Britain and France because they are so close together yet seem so far apart. They are separated by a mere strip of water but cannot agree on its name, the French especially resenting Britain's calling it the English Channel.

The two countries are indeed different. Their peoples respect different values. Their legal codes are different, as are many of their political institutions. They differ in everything from language and culture to cuisine and style, differences that seem to explain everything about them. Why did the French succeed and the British fail in postwar economic recovery? Why did the French oppose British entry into the European Economic Community (EEC)? Why did the British object to a destiny tied to France? It often seems that all observed differences, and the separate paths taken, can be dropped into one or more of three slots – different governmental institutions, different cultures, and different levels of economic development.

Although France and Britain are both parliamentary systems, their political resemblance stops just about there. Britain's head of state is a monarch, France's an elected president who for over twenty years has also been head of government. British tradition (stereotyped) provides for two parties, the French for several. Britain's tradition is liberal, with no place for a Communist Party. France's tradition is radical-egalitarian, and the Communist Party has been a significant political force for more than three decades. The British civil service is humanistic – professional but not professionalized. France's is as opposite as can be, with the *corps, grandes écoles,* and a highly technocratic orientation. British government is decentralized, with very strong local authorities; French government is Paris, with weak local institutions. This characterization is part stereotype, part misrepresentation by overemphasis, and part plain wrong. But for years it has explained a great deal of observed behavior in what frequently seems a parlor game of comparison.

Where political institutions do not reach, culture may. The French Revolution can be considered both a formative experience and a great lever in the work of explanation. It poses aristocracy against democracy, tradition and individualism against change and collectivism.[1] How stereotyped is this assessment? How good is any explanation that can explain everything in general yet offer little in particular?

That the two countries had such different paths of postwar recovery is both a fact needing explanation and a source for explaining other phenomena. France mastered the tools of growth while Britain floundered in a lack of discovery or acceptance of the new *tutelle.* The fact, however, is contrary to reasonable expectations. Of all the Allies except the United States, Britain was considered by many most likely to succeed. Through the forge of war political and economic powers were consolidated to defeat Germany. The Continental economies were distorted by war and occupation; much infrastructure was destroyed. Britain, neither invaded nor occupied, retained economic control. Moreover, a moderate Socialist government was elected in 1945 with a mandate to plan for economic well-being. Why then did Britain lag behind France, Germany, and even Italy and others? British analysts themselves looked to the French differences for explanations, especially to French planning and a "techno-bureaucracy" willing and able to coerce people and industry toward positive economic outcomes.[2] The contrast was between the British preference for compromise at the expense of efficiency and the French stress on accomplishment. Culturally, the British simply needed to be more French if they were to succeed.

British analysts were joined by French and American counterparts in concluding that France was the model for getting things done in the modern world of economic development. There had to be greater state activity and central planning.[3] The 1960s gave incontrovertible proof. Even those analysts who denied that the planning differences were especially great still accepted the premise of cultural, institutional, and economic contrast, but they saw the two countries converging.[4] They saw the French surrendering some state control to the private sector to provide more incentives to business innovation; they saw the British moving at the same time toward the French model; both would thus be left with mixed economies. Although their convergence theory seems to have had no place for Margaret Thatcher or François Mitterrand, they still saw convergence.

Another element supporting a theory of convergence is technology and its common requirements, which even British cultural idiosyncracies cannot evade.[5] Technology imposes administrative values of rationality and efficiency on the most humanistic of governments if they are at all committed to general economic growth. Cultural differences do not stop countries from surrendering some features of democracy to technocracy. Expertise is required to confront complexity. From whatever cultural or governmental or administrative starting point, convergence is the tendency, but not a convergence of growing mutually together. It is convergence toward the French model.

FRENCH SUPERIORITY AND BRITISH FAILURE

There is almost universal agreement that French performance has been superior to British, and the secret of the success of the French, most concur, has been in their pursuit of economic development through planning. One direction of inquiry has pursued the organization of French macroeconomic planning to discern how the French made it work.[6] A second direction of inquiry has dissected British attempts at planning to see why those attempts did not improve economic performance.

The case for French superiority

The case for French superiority is based on two ideas. First, analysts perceive that centralized, rational planning exists in France and is effective. Identification is descriptive, effectiveness is judgmental. Even critics of the French system tend to accept the description.

Second, French superiority is judged to be the product of experts more competent than their counterparts in Britain, and in France these experts enjoy more autonomy to impose the results of their planning and analysis. The French technocrats have the power they both need and deserve to assure the society of favorable outcomes.

Centralization and planning: the popular image. France, social scientists have asserted repeatedly, sustains Jacobin traditions as the basis of state legitimacy. This centralization has referred both to the dominance of Paris over the rest of France and to the concentration of authority among a small number of élite decision makers in the capital.

In the last two decades, the image of centralization has been enhanced by the evolution of "rational planning" and French advances in high technology. The *étatisme* praised by Andrew Shonfield referred to a centralized state where policy emerged from a unified central administration.[7] Policy was the product of integrated planning; inefficiency, on economic criteria, was eschewed; the state marshaled resources on behalf of defined goals and coherent implementation. The proof of success lay in high rates of

economic growth, low unemployment, and general economic development. The symbol of potential success – and
of French international leadership – was to be found in
the advanced technologies, especially nuclear power and
civil aviation.[8] The mystique of achievement in high technology, in fact, evolved as essential evidence of the legitimacy of a French state still governed through central control, but increasingly by technocrats.

Most analysts of France assume that important, if not all,
French decisions are made in Paris and that Paris is, some-
how, a monolith of decision making. Suzanne Berger, for
example, writes that "power is distributed in such a way in
France today that only the center can exercise effective
controls."[9] Shonfield says, "The French can plan easily, because they have a system and an apparatus ready-made to
take up the task of planning." This apparatus, he explains,
involves "effective centralized control over economic policy."[10] State ownership, public expenditure and investment, presidential authority, and central planning and decision making are offered as indicators of central power.

There are two important objections to this monolithic
view. Much has been written in the last decade calling into
question the assumption that real power is concentrated in
Paris.[11] Urbanization outside Paris, as well as the growth
of leftist power at the municipal level, has helped demon-
strate that significant political choices can reside locally and
that Paris does not necessarily dominate all of France. But
within Paris itself there has been much less refinement of
analysis concerning the fragmentation of decision-making
authority.

Divisions of authority in Paris continue to be understood
primarily as competition between elected structures (particularly the Assemblée Nationale) and administrative and
bureaucratic organs. This view is adopted by structural-
functionalists,[12] political economists,[13] and scholars em-
phasizing a relationship between culture and political
structure. Subtle analysts have observed competition be-

tween traditional bureaucracies staffed politically and new bureaucracies staffed with technocrats endowed with new educational preparation,[14] but this refinement, too, emphasizes the quest, often successful, for coherence in central authority.

Even critics of French planning have accepted the assertion of centralization. They have doubted whether the planning is either rational or democratic, but not whether it is the product of a unified administration. Stephen Cohen, for example, has argued that French planning is incoherent, but above all because of competition between public and private power and the inherent weakness of a mixed economy.[15] Public authorities cannot control many forces, he has said, including inflation, international prices, war, and trade embargoes.[16] Most important, as Cohen and later Jack Hayward demonstrated, planning is political and therefore cannot achieve technical elegance. But they have not doubted that planning in France is centralized, or that it sets forth a general national direction.

There are three underlying concepts for French planning: (1) The exercise is centralized, centralizing, and rational; (2) planning is participatory, encouraging input from interested parties and sectors; (3) there may be a need for present sacrifice on behalf of future gain. John McArthur and Bruce Scott, among others, have criticized the participatory mechanisms for industry,[17] and Cohen has questioned the distribution of sacrifice and gain. However, the examination of these features has been confined to planning in specific sectors or for particular economic policies. They have not been considered in light of public works or large-scale government projects, and they have not been tested with respect to activity controlled within the public sector. Above all, perhaps, French efforts in high technology and prestige projects have been peculiarly immune to analysis. Criticisms of French planning have pointed to weaknesses in the mixed economy (hence the dialogue between Shonfield and Hayward), but a failure to coordinate among responsible public agencies has been ignored. Peter Hall has argued that the bureaucracy can indeed be divided and that government apparatus is fragmented, but he has not yet given substance to the claim.[18]

The case for British failure

Two basic arguments support the case for British inferiority – for the contrast between France's centralized, rational planning and the British government's weaker authority over the economy. First, Britain is understood to have a fundamental commitment to pluralism. Pluralism, in the British setting, encourages democratic participation, whose product is indecision, delay, and even paralysis.

The second argument, like the first, emerges as a criticism of a traditional British virtue. The stable institutions, which so many have venerated, are found guilty of generating a stagnating incrementalism where "muddling through" is a national value. The British prefer amateurism to expertise, and they utilize generalists who hold tenaciously to fixed government positions for job security instead of professional specialists eager for accomplishment and promotion.

British pluralism and participation. One of Britain's apparently fine institutional accomplishments on behalf of democracy has been regarded by many political observers as a grave handicap in economic development. The British commitment to compromise and consensus can lead to stalemate. Samuel Beer, and later Jack Hayward, called the British phenomenon "pluralistic stagnation."[19] Andrew Shonfield complained of government operating at "arm's length," suffering from "inhibitions on the use of public power in the private sector"; he went on to accuse the British of having a "doctrine of anti-planning."[20]

The assault on British pluralism has been different from the critique of American pluralism that preceded it. In the

United States, objections to pluralism emerged because a favorable disposition toward pluralism seemed to legitimize decision making that gave great advantage to narrow and wealthy interests at the expense of the general public.[21] Those who could hire professional lobbyists obviously influenced decisions much more than those who could not afford such services; those who enjoyed leisure time to organize enjoyed great political advantage over those whose work denied them comparable opportunities. Public policy, U.S. critics charged, fell victim to the objectives of big business, big agriculture, and big labor; the public interest found no spokesman.[22]

The critics of British pluralism observed similar interest-group influences, but they worried more about the decline of public authority. A government unwilling to impose its will became merely an additional negotiating partner in the tripartism of government, industry, and unionized labor. Analysts of the U.S. experience worried that a decline in public authority was the product of a decline in the legitimacy of governments bereft of adequate popular participation. British critics of pluralism, by contrast, never doubted that their arrangements of tripartism were "participatory" (though it was a circumscribed participation); they took exception, above all, to their system's inefficiency.

The attitude toward pluralism in Britain has been reflected more broadly as an attitude toward participation itself. Whereas U.S. critics of pluralism called for greater popular participation – greater opportunities for those traditionally excluded from the political process to become involved – British analysts complained that participation was an obstacle to progress. In the march of economic progress, they reasoned, the French had demonstrated well the value of ignoring unofficial spokesmen and occasional citizen groups. Activists outside formal structures of unions, industry, and government (or parties) were held by the

French to be representatives of particular wills; only the government could articulate the general will. British observers, including Shonfield and Hayward, wanted to copy the French model in dealing with participation, just as they wanted to absorb the French approach to planning.

After centuries evolving institutions for a public role in decision making, Britain now was criticized for such institutionalized participation, especially in public hearings, because it stood in the path of economic and technological progress and in the way of the national will. It was not that any decision-making authority had been removed from government but rather that public opinion could be influenced by expressions of pressure-group sentiment that the government did not seem to have sufficient good sense to prevent.

The British plainly were jealous of the ease with which the French apparently went about their business. There could be no debate about pluralism in France because there was no pretension about participation. There could be no reversal of policy owing to public opinion because public opinion was not permitted to mobilize opposition to government. The opposition political parties might prevent the implementation of policy, but not over economic growth or technological development. Only the policy means could be disputed, for consensus reigned on the objectives. And on public works as a means, the government enjoyed consensus from all official quarters.

According to this view of pluralism and participation, an important British ideological flaw is a commitment to including actors outside government in deliberations over policy. The difficulty, critics have argued, resides not in insufficient representation but in too much. "Conflict is minimized," Hayward writes, "at the cost of innovation."[23] This view assumes that a governmental exercise of authority would yield better outcomes (on the French model) and that the decision-making process – not the international or even domestic economic or political or social conditions, or the structure of participation – has been the chief culprit in British economic failures. The view assumes, too, that the French government does legitimately express the general will and that so would a British government with the courage to act decisively.

British stability and economic stagnation. Another of the most esteemed attributes of British government has been two-party stability and institutional continuity. Few stereotypes are more widely held or more universally revered. Yet British critics of economic performance have argued that continuity often has meant a lack of innovation and an inability to change course or try new ideas. Once again a British attribute appears to be a characterological flaw.

The traditional view of British politics, shared by Samuel Beer, S. E. Finer,[24] and David Butler and Donald Stokes,[25] among others, has been criticized by party analysts who see an erosion of support and a decline in membership for Labour and the Conservatives.[26] Fewer British citizens are participating in the electoral process; the 1974 general elections left a power balance precariously suspended among the Liberals, the Ulster Unionists, and the Scottish Nationalists. The slippage of these other parties in 1979 was accompanied by further decline in the support of the two largest parties, and even those who describe the system without full acknowledgment of the multi-party phenomena complain of disproportionate representation and illegitimate government.[27] The startling rise of the Social Democratic Party in 1980 could only mystify traditional analysts.

These criticisms of the British party system imply a growing weakness of government because of the questionable basis of power. Hence the concentration of potential government in the hands of two weakening parties can only contribute to the inability of government to plan and implement. The parties stand as a barrier to innovation. A more serious doubt is raised in the continuity of the civil service. Shonfield and Hayward both complain that the British limit the role of technical experts who would improve the quality of decisions.[28] Moreover, according to Hayward, even the few well-trained civil servants available do not participate early enough in the process because "administrative and interest group consensus [is] treated as a prerequisite of planning."[29] Beer observes that despite the civil service reforms proposed by the Fulton Committee, "the social origins of those entering the Administrative class have remained fairly narrow."[30] He encourages efforts to stimulate the presence of more technical skill in the administration of British government.

The weakness of expertise in British government is partner to the entrenched influence of civil servants who control decision areas. This critical assessment suggests that as civil servants guarantee the continuity of government they also assure the absence of imagination and insistence upon ill-informed, politically insensitive, and technically unsound proposals. It also assumes that French experts understand mixed economies and the future better than British generalists and that government entrusted to technocracy is preferable to "a highly compartmentalized system in which business, administrative and trade union leaders [negotiate] with each other compromises that frequently [break] down once one move[s] out of the consensus-creating committee room into the real world of confrontation between conflicting interests."[31] British analysts, then, have believed that French specialists are more realistic than British civil servants and that "elite consensus thanks to the authoritative interlocking economic directorate of those who [head] the major private and public corporations, the key administrative corps and ministries, with the *cabinet ministériel*"[32] (to the obvious exclusion of labor), is preferable to negotiation and compromise with a broader base of concerned citizens.

A CRITICAL ASSESSMENT OF FRENCH
SUPERIORITY AND BRITISH FAILURE

Evidence and inference

It is surprising to discover that much of the criticism leveled at Britain, and the praise bestowed on France, derives from generalizations, stereotypes, and single cases.[33] Comparisons have been undertaken through the analysis of policy sectors (narrow arenas of government decision making, such as transportation, employment and incomes, industrial policy, etc.), but less through the examination of specific policies; there have been surveys of legislation and formal planning apparatus, but the systematic comparison of problem solving on similar issues is absent; most comparisons outside planning are implicit.

The stereotypes have been reinforced by scholars whose objectives appear at least partially ideological, for state authority could not be promoted in Britain if French control were judged a failure, nor could a demand for change be sustained if British economic development were deemed successful. Only the combination of French success and British failure, based on French superiority, could support the case.[34]

The case, in part at least, must be judged on its merits. A systematic empirical comparison of problem solving in one public sector during one period of time can help pose appropriate questions. In dealing with a common problem, did the French forecast the future more reliably than the British? Did they coordinate the public and private sectors more efficiently? Did they mobilize government activity more successfully to assure greater economic development? Did they better understand the public interest?

Civil aviation: an ideal case

An ideal problem for comparing French and British planning would be one in high technology, where both countries have counted on rapid advancement to sustain economic growth. Comparisons of one industry (e.g., steel, electronics, textiles) involve numerous uncontrollable variations because there can be no reliable starting point at which the conditions for each respective national industry are the same. But problems that are defined internationally, where developments in one country cannot possibly escape developments in the other, impose control on critical variables. The construction of advanced aircraft and civil aviation infrastructure fit into this category.

Civil aviation, unlike most other industries, effectively halted during World War II. Countries at war did not move many civilians by air. Military landing fields were built, but there was no construction of civil airports, and airplanes were built to fight. Both Britain and France had begun to develop international air travel before the war, especially for transporting mail, but both began the postwar era without a commercial route structure and effectively without infrastructure.[35] Both set as national priorities the restoration and development of air travel.

The London–Paris route quickly established itself as the busiest in Europe. Whatever the rest of their respective air traffic networks, both Britain and France required similar infrastructure to accommodate the traffic they shared. Plans for Heathrow and Orly were developed between 1944 and 1946; through the 1950s both London and Paris operated two international airports, and between 1957 and 1959 both laid plans for a third.

Planners in Britain and France, working in the same technology at the same time, set out very similar estimates of needs that appeared to be based on very similar traffic forecasts. They employed almost identical criteria for site selection. Planners in both countries owed their jobs to government, not the private sector, and the governments shared assumptions about a responsibility to cater to the needs of a "traveling public." They defined airport and aircraft development as technical problems, and they set out similar procedures and criteria for solving them.

Suiting the stereotypes

Both Britain and France pinned postwar hopes on the development of high technology. Both chose the strategy of nationalized industries. In civil aviation, both operated nationalized airlines, and both brought their principal international airports under public authorities with grants of significant operating autonomy. French governments have pointed proudly, and analysts casually but often, to the contrast in achievement, whether in the air with the military Mirage and the commercial Airbus or on the ground with Charles de Gaulle Airport. The British failed to build a lasting or internationally popular military plane; their contribution to the TriStar L1011 broke Rolls Royce; and the third London airport remained in bitter dispute a quarter century after first plans were introduced for its construction. In the realm of stereotypes, there are few if any examples more obvious or apparently more satisfying. The French built their planes and airports; the British did not. The French established symbols of high technology achievement that enabled them to embark on substantial international consulting and sales; the British boasted only overcrowded facilities and a dying aircraft industry.

The example of civil aviation is particularly salient, then, precisely because the respective governments have invested so much energy and money and because the outcomes in the 1980s seem to conform to the national stereotypes. The strength of the stereotypes has even encouraged interpretations that convert similarities into differences. The French, it is commonly argued, interpreted the development of civil aviation as an opportunity to gain prestige for technological know-how and as a means of limiting U.S. domination; the British, in contrast, inclined toward modest and incremental development, often in cooperation with the United States and in order to preserve an economic sphere of manufacture and trade. Hence, so the argument runs, the French built grand and costly airports and promoted the construction of aircraft on the technological frontier of the industry; the British permitted criteria of environmental amenities and cost-effectiveness to control development.

The French and British, it seemed, gave opposite priorities to prestige and profit. The explanations fit perfectly the general hypotheses about planning and economic development. These analyses assume that French and British élites reflect their respective institutions and cultures so thoroughly that they envision solutions to common problems differently and prefer different policies and different processes. The consistency of technology may occasionally overcome these differences, but the instances are rare and the differences must be assumed at the outset.

REAPPRAISING THE STEREOTYPES

During the same time period, officials in both Britain and France defined the same problem, the need for an additional international airport for the capital city. The contrasting outcomes in the two cases support the broader contrasts between the two countries, but detailed assessments raise complex questions about measuring success and failure. A focus on the process, rather than the outcomes, affords the opportunity to reconsider whether in fostering development France is indeed so different from Britain.

British and French officials also worked during this period to solve together a commonly defined problem. The task – the development, construction, and marketing of supersonic transport – absorbed the attention of Europe's leading aircraft industries; a problem whose solution eluded the richer and presumably more capable Americans was solved by British and French specialists through intimate cooperation sustained over more than a decade. The Concorde experience, a fully joint venture with equal measures of French and British personnel, equipment, and political and financial support, casts doubt on the overriding importance of cultures.

If the cultural or historical explanations of contrast between Britain and France were correct, the problem definition and planning procedures for construction of third international airports in London and Paris should have been as different as the outcomes. The French and British should have valued the accomplishment of these projects differently, should have used different criteria to design and assess them, and should have assimilated them into their respective political and economic systems according to their own national peculiarities and priorities. Furthermore, the national differences should have made highly sophisticated, prestigious, and incalculably expensive joint enterprise impossible. Yet in both instances, the approach of French and British élites has been nearly the same. An explanation for these similarities founded on a technological imperative, which may seem seductive if not obvious, cannot address the fact that in these cases technology has afforded a broad range of choice in procedure and strategies. To explain the contradiction of logical expectations we must look further. Whatever the superficial contrasts suggesting confirmation of the stereotypes, the conventional wisdom does not hold up well in these critical cases.

Of course, it will not be enough to identify preponderant similarities, however much they contradict a conventional wisdom. The stereotypes, however inaccurate, were born not of witlessness but of exaggerated generality. The contrasting outcomes in the airport cases do require their own explanations. It is one thing to discover that the traditional explanations have been wrong, but quite another to discover what explanations are right. There are differences of consequence between Britain and France, but not necessarily those traditionally recognized, for the generalizations do not explain specific instances, and too rarely have specific cases been the focus of systematic comparison. A greater approximation of truth thus may derive from accurate and specific descriptions and subsequent reinterpretation. Such an approximation of truth may then expose more clearly how indeed different countries deal with common technologies and common goals.

2

The Parisian white elephant

Charles de Gaulle Airport, rationalized in part as a response to the technological requirements of Concorde,[1] is in the 1980s a monument to technical hubris and uncoordinated central planning. It is flawed conceptually and in its technical execution. It is the product of political choice more than technical plan, and despite its apparent success when contrasted with the commercial failure of Concorde, the airport's glamour cannot hide fully its own fundamental irrationalities.

Rational planning, in the French context, often degenerates into the rationalization of planning. Explanations remote from the reality of technique, politics, or actual events can emerge to deflect criticism of French accomplishment, criticism that is little tolerated in France because of the relationship between state legitimacy and technical achievement.[2] The analysis that follows contrasts official French explanations, as reported in interviews, the media, and official documents (although often they are not very accessible to the general public), with a more accurate rendition culled from private interviews and unofficial and private documents. The story of Charles de Gaulle Airport bears witness to failures both in French rationality and in the social science paradigms that have characterized the French state.

CENTRALIZED RATIONAL PLANNING

Official explanations for building

Aéroport de Paris, the autonomous public authority that owns and operates all nonmilitary airports within fifty kilometers of Notre Dame Cathedral, has rewritten some of the documentary history (observable in official but formally secret files) in order to persuade both French and foreign customers contracting consulting services that Charles de Gaulle Airport was the product of vision and rational planning. The major problems of the airport at the end of the 1970s – overpurchase of land, excess capacity, troubled neighbors, inefficient access, maldistribution of traffic, air traffic conflict with Le Bourget – might have been foreseeable in a rational and open process. But Charles de Gaulle Airport was planned and is managed with great secrecy; the French public and even responsible French officials often are ignorant of the intentions and operating procedures of Aéroport de Paris.

Official explanations for the development of Charles de Gaulle Airport focus on two necessities: that of meeting the demand of forecast traffic and that of providing facilities able to accommodate supersonic transport. Aéroport de Paris planners claim that neither Le Bourget, where Charles Lindbergh landed the *Spirit of St. Louis,* nor Orly, which opened its first modern terminal in 1961, could grow enough to handle traffic that would double every five years. Although more terminal space would be provided, urban encroachment prevented additional runway construction without great disturbance in nearby neighborhoods, and the increase in passenger traffic would mean an increase in aircraft movements. Aéroport de Paris needed a site large enough to insulate an airport from encroachment, and just such a land parcel happened to exist northeast of Paris. An airport for the future would be built there.

Aéroport de Paris forecasts were simple extrapolations

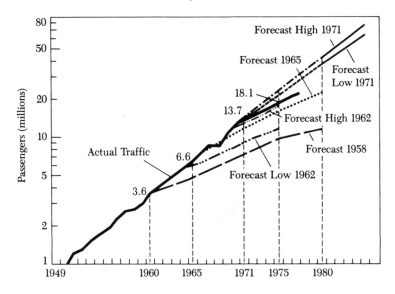

Figure 2.1. Aéroport de Paris forecasts of growth in air travel. (N.B.: The y-axis of this graph is logarithmic, rather than linear.) Reprinted by permission of the publisher from Elliot J. Feldman and Jerome Milch, Technocracy versus Democracy: The Comparative Politics of International Airports *(Boston, Mass.: Auburn House Publishing Co., 1982).*

of growth in the late 1950s (see Fig. 2.1). No allowance was made for growth in aircraft size. Thus Aéroport de Paris foresaw an increase in the number of planes directly proportionate to increases in the number of passengers. Runway capacities, limited by the capabilities of air traffic control systems, would be inadequate by the end of the 1960s. No sooner was construction under way on Orly (in 1954) than the search for a third site in the Paris region began, and when the Paris-Nord site was chosen in 1957 (at Roissy-en-France for what became Charles de Gaulle), Aéroport de Paris launched studies concerning the location of a possible fourth airport. Hence Orly was not conceived as the long-term solution to Paris's airport requirements, nor even at the outset was Charles de Gaulle. French planners never doubted the reliability of their forecasts or their responsibility to provide facilities consistent with anticipated traffic demand.

Additional runways assumed a constant technology growing on a strictly quantitative dimension. Concorde, however, posed other demands. Not only would runways perhaps need to be longer; they would also need to be far from populated areas, for the engine thrust necessary to lift off and to set down supersonic aircraft would generate intolerable noise for nearby residents. And Orly's terminal design could not cope with the anticipated wingspan of the new plane. The technological imperative – that Concorde be built as the logical next step in civil aviation, imposing in the process certain requirements – encouraged Aéroport de Paris officials to construct a new "environmental" airport that would have sufficient land to guarantee future development and would enjoy buffer zones protecting neighbors from noise.

The unofficial story

The official explanations for the development of a third international airport in Paris emphasize three points: (1) Charles de Gaulle Airport was the product of rational planning in response to the natural forces of the market and of technology; (2) a new airport would require large quantities of land to insulate against urban encroachment; and (3) Paris-Nord would be the third major airport in the region, with a fourth one a distinct possibility.[3]

There are many reasons to doubt the official story: The design of the airport eliminated a buffer zone despite the acquisition of a land parcel one-third the size of all Paris; Le Bourget Airport was closed to commercial traffic in 1977, a move that left only two international airports in the Paris region; traffic into the 1970s fell significantly below the forecasts. On the one hand, it could be argued that these contradictions resulted merely from error. On the other hand, the design of the airport suggests that the acquisition of a large parcel was in response not to technology, nor to anticipated demand, nor even to anticipated urban encroachment. And if the airport was not designed to satisfy any of these imperatives, then surely other reasons lay behind original planning.

In fact, the idea of Paris-Nord began with the District of Paris, not with the technical planners of Aéroport de Paris. It was conceived as an alternative to Le Bourget, not an addition, and it was proposed initially without reference to traffic forecasts or to new technology. In the first comprehensive plans for the Paris Region after World War II, Le Bourget was designated to become a park (a plan substantially modified through Aéroport de Paris's pressure in the 1970s).[4] District Director Gibel's planning team identified a large land parcel further out from central Paris than the land proposed for parks, industry, and residences, and Gibel personally suggested to Aéroport de Paris an exchange, Le Bourget for a site offering an opportunity for a new airport. Within eight months, in late 1957, Aéroport de Paris agreed to give up Le Bourget in exchange for a site to the northeast.

The site for Paris-Nord, drawing land from seven communes in two departments – all beyond Paris's municipal boundaries – was rich in beetroot and wheat. Large mechanized farms were operated by only fifty-two principal owners, and only one set of farm buildings occupied space on the 7,670 acres, which were surrounded by tiny villages. The land had been used to train Napoleon's army and lay on the invasion route from the north. These historical uses, plus the absence of water, had kept the land, known as the "Plains of France," empty while Paris grew in every other direction. The village with easiest access to the metropolitan center, Roissy-en-France, was less than sixteen miles from the heart of Paris.

Site selection was simple. The land at Roissy-en-France (as the site and later the airport temporarily became known) was the largest, closest parcel identified by drawing concentric circles around Notre Dame Cathedral. A comparable parcel in any other direction would have required doubling the distance from the center, and no other site was already linked to Paris by a major highway. A site outside the Paris region for a national airport was never considered, and in any event Paris authorities held an overwhelming monopoly on airport expertise and necessarily controlled the analysis. Although numerous sites were studied and compared, planners never perceived any choice.

Only after Gibel's proposal was accepted, a site had been chosen, and master planning had begun did a rationale for Paris-Nord emerge. When the master plan was ready in 1963, after six years of calculations, the government condemned the land, authorizing expropriation by declaring it committed to a public utility. Only then did the French learn that Orly, planned after World War II as Paris's great airport to share service with Le Bourget, would not be sufficient for future needs and would not, indeed, even be Paris's great airport. Orly would acquire a second major terminal, but Orly's estimated capacity, according to French planners, would never top seventeen million passengers per year. Paris-Nord would be able to handle fifty million or more.

The District of Paris had proposed the site but had not appreciated how much land Aéroport de Paris would seek to possess. The Ministry of Finance had not been aware of how much the project would cost; the Ministry of Defense had not examined potential conflict with an air force base at Creil, beyond minimum assurances for continued operation; the Ministry of Equipment had not considered potential pressure on the highway system; and the director-general of the Société Nationale des Chemins de Fer (SNCF), managing the nation's railroads, had not been consulted at all about rail access between the airport and Paris or between the new airport and Orly. The site was announced, the land condemned, and the preliminary master plans approved before any of these parties became involved in decisions affecting the new airport. Aéroport de Paris specified the size and shape of the land parcel without Ministry of Finance approval, even though Finance would bear ultimate responsibility for expropriation. Indeed, no participating agency, including the Régie Autonome des Transports Parisiens (Métro) (RATP), who would share responsibility for access, was allowed into the planning of the airport until the essential decisions already were firm.

The evidence is clear that the decision committing the largest land parcel in the Paris region remaining undeveloped after 1950 was not coordinated with implicated agencies, was not determined through economically rational criteria, and did not reflect unified administration. Not only did planning take place outside the Commissariat Général du Plan and the Ministry of Finance, the two crucial centralizing agencies; airport design, we shall soon see, contradicted national plans.

Land acquisition

Two claims have characterized the official story on land acquisition. First, French authorities emphasize that they developed a rational plan for land use and acquired a parcel to meet specific requirements. Second, they distinguish their proceedings from experience in other countries, where great conflict erupted over expropriation.[5] The French, they insist, acquired land *à l'amiable,* in friendly agreement with landowners.

It took Aéroport de Paris three years to complete the acquisition of land. Although officially they planned an airport and acquired enough land to satisfy the plan, unofficially there were only tentative designs and estimates when the airport boundaries were specified. Aéroport de

Paris took all the land it could get without taking homes, a step that would have generated conflict and, more important, would have been more expensive.[6]

The owners of the land formed a syndicate to negotiate price. Over the centuries numerous complex and often informal transactions had divided and traded parcels, so that ownership corresponded little to units actually worked. The syndicate decided to seek a single price for the entire land package, a solution also preferable to Ministry of Finance agents responsible for assessment, because the syndicate would sort out compensation rights and differences in the quality (and hence value) of parcels. Nevertheless, such cooperation did not induce rapid agreement on price, and the syndicate president, also president of the Technical Institute for Beetroot and one of the most powerful agricultural spokesmen in France, drove the price constantly higher.

The final agreement for acquisition was worked out personally between the president of Aéroport de Paris and the president of the Association of Owners and Farmers of the Region Northeast of Paris. They agreed to a price well below a price appropriate for industrial use (in accordance with French expropriation law) but significantly higher than the top assessment of Ministry of Finance agents; approval required the personal intervention of the minister of finance (then Valéry Giscard d'Estaing) to override the judgment of the Administration des Domaines, the responsible agency within the Finance Ministry. Aéroport de Paris, which would be paying for the land, recognized that regardless of price the land represented a small fraction of overall costs and should not, therefore, become an obstacle for meeting the 1972 target for opening the airport. For the state, however, such a high price set a precedent inflating the value of other land in cases where the state would have to pay. Indeed, later negotiations in the area involving property for other purposes included constant reference to the airport expropriation. *A*

l'amiable referred more to the state's desire to avoid controversy than to a fair price determined through the consistent and rational process of land evaluation for which the
Administration des Domaines took great pride.

Acquisition in fact occurred in two phases. Initially,
Aéroport de Paris acquired 7,413 acres (3,000 hectares).
When plans were developed, however, conflict arose with
Air France over the location of the engine-testing zone.
Air France did not want to taxi across the airport expanse
from Terminal I (see Map 2.1). Aéroport de Paris agreed
to acquire an additional 257 acres (104 hectares) adjacent
to the village of Roissy-en-France in order to accommodate Air France.

The second acquisition resulted in part from the exclusion of Air France in the planning of the airport. Not until
1968, when Pierre Donatien Cot moved from Aéroport de
Paris to Air France and Louis Lesieux (formerly director
of Aéroport de Paris) retired at Air France, did the national flag carrier join regular consultations on the airport's development.[7] The second acquisition also may have
resulted from political concerns, for the additional 257 acres
effectively surrounded the village of Roissey-en-France and
exposed it to the airport's noisiest activities. It was easier
to add a small section once construction had begun than
to display an original master plan jeopardizing the survival
of the village.

The overall land acquisition was facilitated by two overriding factors. The French government was willing to pay
as much as four times the agricultural market value of the
land (utilizing various compensatory devices for inconvenience and relocation), and the parcels were very large.
Only one owner objected to the settlement through legal
proceedings.

The Ministry of Finance was not easily persuaded that
so much land was needed or that the price should be so
high. Orly Airport would occupy only 4,200 acres, and financial settlements were generous but not apparently ex-

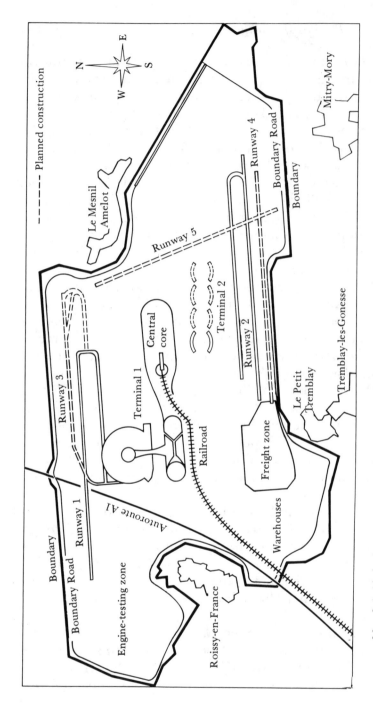

Map 2.1. Sixth plan for Charles de Gaulle Airport, 1974. Redrawn from Aéroport de Paris map, March 1973.

cessive. Aéroport de Paris enlisted Gibel's successor, Paul Delouvrier, to help persuade the government of the need for the land. He was shown plans for five round terminals and at least four runways. With faith in the technical skill and integrity of Aéroport de Paris, Paris's chief planner never questioned the plans.

The airport design and land use: official needs

When most passengers think of an airport they think only of a terminal building and perhaps also a runway. To an airport operator, however, the facility includes taxiways, aprons, cargo areas, control tower, parking facilities, maintenance areas, hangars, warehouses, and testing zones. The design of an airport involves the integration of many different functions, for which terminal design is but one feature. Although Charles de Gaulle Airport means to most people a round terminal with moving ramps and suspended tubes, the airport's design depends more on runway location and air traffic control.

Aéroport de Paris officials argued that quantities of land were required for the new airport in order to prevent encroachment, anticipate demand, and accommodate Concorde. Concorde, they thought, would pose three problems: It would need long runways, its wingspan would make it difficult for fingers to reach out from the terminal to the plane's door for passengers, and it would produce disturbing noise. The first problem would be solved simply by paving longer runways. The second problem would be solved by arranging for the plane to park away from the main terminal, a plan that evolved into the airport's satellite system: Passengers pass underground from the main terminal to a mini-terminal for actual embarkation. The third problem would depend on positioning the runways.

The design of an airport begins with runways.[8] To limit noise and achieve an "environmental airport,"[9] the areas where most noise is generated must be isolated from pop-

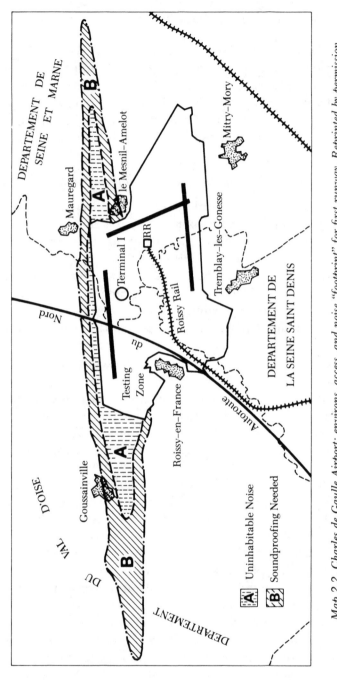

Map 2.2. *Charles de Gaulle Airport: environs, access, and noise "footprint" for first runway. Reprinted by permission of the publisher from Elliot J. Feldman and Jerome Milch, Technocracy versus Democracy: The Comparative Politics of International Airports (Boston, Mass.: Auburn House Publishing Co., 1982).*

ulated areas. Planes are noisiest when engines are revved for taking off or testing or throttled for landing. Hence the quietest airport would embalm runways and engine-testing areas within open, unpopulated land, and runways would point in the direction of the least-populated areas surrounding the airport.

If Charles de Gaulle Airport were to make the environment a principal criterion for its design, then the runways would lie east–west (parallel to Paris) in the center of the airport, with all other facilities and land surrounding them. Parallel runways, separated for operational safety by at least one mile,[10] could site the engine-testing zone between them. All noise would then be concentrated in the center. Charles de Gaulle's parallel runways do lie east–west, though as much because of the prevailing winds on the European continent as because of the position's relationship to Paris.[11] The runways, however, are located at the peripheries of the airport, with the head of Runway 1 facing the largest populated community in the area, Goussainville (see Map 2.2). The engine-testing zone, attached to the western corner of the airport, is on the doorstep of Roissy-en-France. The design maximizes noise and belies the argument that the airport was meant to be an environmental facility accommodating the supersonic transport. And plans for Runways 3 and 4 require further land acquisition beyond the present airport boundaries, without adequate separation for safe parallel, simultaneous use.

Airport design and land use: unofficial explanations

If the 7,670 acres did not include a buffer zone to isolate noise, why was so much land required? Aéroport de Paris officials concede that their most optimistic forecasts of the late 1960s (even when later revised upward) indicated that Orly, with an additional terminal and runway (for which land had long since been acquired), could combine with Le Bourget to meet traffic demand until at least 1990. Two terminals and two runways at a new airport, even with the closing of Le Bourget, would suffice for the most extreme forecasts of the 1970s until the year 2000.[12] Moreover, Terminal I was built in the northwest corner of the airport and Terminal II subsequently was built in the southeast. The entire center and all of the northeast sections have remained empty, save for a rail station that deserves a separate discussion (see the following section).

While Paul Delouvrier was being persuaded by plans that called for five round terminals (capable of handling between fifty and seventy-five million passengers per year with great comfort), Aéroport de Paris was in fact laying plans more to guarantee income than to meet traffic demand. Operating on an autonomous budget with a charter provision requiring full commercial exploitation of airport operations,[13] Aéroport de Paris planned warehouses, storage depots, light industry, and a commercial complex of hotels, banks, cinemas, shops, laundromats, restaurants, and so on. The airport was meant to become the principal shopping center for the northeast region of Paris; land acquired at even the most inflated agricultural prices would be cheap when converted to industrial and commercial use. Aéroport de Paris would use the state's authority and the state's credit to expropriate land at present-use (agricultural) evaluations and exploit the land for "airport-related activities" that would bring in huge rents and concession income. Competitors in appropriate businesses, especially hotels, would have to pay speculative land prices to private owners for less desirable locations. Profits, moreover, would not go back to the state but rather would help the airport authority pay off the interest and principal on the loans from the state for the airport's construction, that is, for the excess land and overdevelopment.

Once the runways were positioned on the airport's peripheries, the land between was effectively sterilized. For reasons of noise, air pollution, and safety, residential potential was eliminated and the land became the permanent property of the airport authority.

The Fifth, Sixth and Seventh National Plans, prepared by the Commissariat Général du Plan to give direction to national development, designate the area northeast of Paris for airport use but specify that commercial and other industrial and residential development should be directed to the east and northwest, toward new towns whose sites were chosen in 1965.[14] The immediate Paris area, the plans declare, should be deconcentrated. The *Aéroport de Paris* projects contravene both the spirit and the letter of the National Plans, but by law the airport authority is sovereign on land it has acquired for airport use. Growth in the airport area, generated by Aéroport de Paris's commercial enterprises and financed by the state and by airport users, promises to obliterate the greenbelt that distinguishes Paris from Picardie to the north.[15] Concentration of activity in the Paris basin will be increased, and Aéroport de Paris alone will profit. Like the land for the new towns, however, the land at Roissy-en-France was taken before any public or interagency discussion of plans and projects was possible.

The provision of access: revising the record

Paris-Nord was linked to Paris by the Autoroute du Nord, which already served Le Bourget, Lille, Brussels, and the ports for London. Government planners recognized the need for a public transportation system and additional roads (see Map 2.3), for the Autoroute du Nord was already approaching rush-hour saturation in the early 1960s.

The desire to make the Roissy facility a monument to French technology and innovation was indicated by the plans for public transportation between the airport and Paris. During the early 1960s the French, like the British, were working on improving speed by reducing friction.

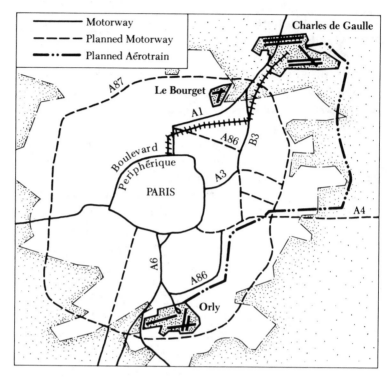

Map 2.3. *Paris with Charles de Gaulle, Le Bourget, and Orly air-ports (* ┼┼┼┼┼ *indicates Roissy-Rail on planned* aérotrain *route to Gare du Nord). Reprinted by permission of the publisher from Elliot J. Feldman and Jerome Milch,* Technocracy versus Democracy: The Comparative Politics of International Airports *(Boston, Mass.: Auburn House Publishing Co., 1982).*

The hovercraft and the hydrofoil, developed on principles of air cushions and reduced contact between stationary and moving surfaces, were emerging as innovative solutions for commuting on the Thames and for crossing the Channel. The French, especially, attempted to adapt the hovercraft principle for a land-based vehicle, the *aérotrain*. The *aérotrain* would ride along a track bed on a cushion of air, which would guarantee a smoother and faster ride than was possible on rails.

All planning for access to the new airport assumed the construction of the *aérotrain*. Routes were sketched on maps linking Paris to the Gare du Nord and linking Orly to Roissy on a circumferential route around the eastern side of the city. Two roads that would lead off the Boulevard Périphérique (not then built either) also were sketched in. No decision was taken in Cabinet or by interested parties (including the SNCF, the RATP, and Aéroport de Paris) concerning which agency would install the *aérotrain* system, although a prototype was developed and by 1971 was being tested near Orléans in the Loire Valley.

Aéroport de Paris has no authority to provide access to its airports, but it does have two preferences. Considerable revenue is associated with parking, so Aéroport de Paris strongly favors the automobile; officials of the new airport, disdainful of the railroad as anachronistic in the supersonic age, also backed the *aérotrain*.

As one senior Aéroport de Paris official ridiculed, "If there are no wheels and tracks the SNCF is not interested." With this view of the SNCF, Aéroport de Paris did not confer with national railroad officials until 1968 (a number of dubious official – but still private – documents to the contrary notwithstanding), after construction of the airport facilities already had begun. Construction of the Boulevard Périphérique took much longer than expected, retarding the construction of the feeder roads until the late 1970s and early 1980s. The technology of the *aérotrain* ran into difficulties with escalating development costs and application. Aéroport de Paris's commitment to the newest – and most expensive – technology, and the absence of any committee or agency to coordinate intermodal transportation, destined Roissy to open with only the direct access that existed before the airport was built, the Autoroute du Nord.

Problems with the *aérotrain* were fourfold. First, the vehicle had numerous technological difficulties associated with stabilizing its movement along a path while riding on air.

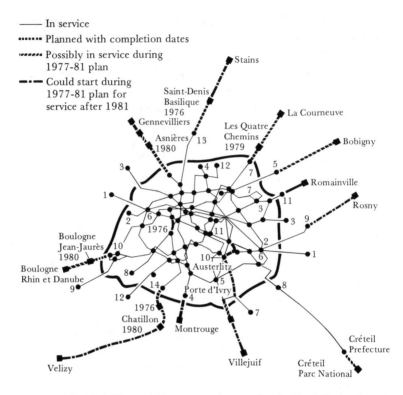

—— In service

•••••• Planned with completion dates

⚋⚋⚋ Possibly in service during 1977–81 plan

⚊•⚊ Could start during 1977–81 plan for service after 1981

Map 2.4. Planned Metro network expansion for Paris Basin. Redrawn from RATP: Plan d'entreprise, 1977–1981 (Paris: RATP, n.d.), p. 29.

Second, the vehicle generated much more noise than a conventional rail system because of the engine thrust required to build up speed. Third, the circumferential route linking the two airports led villages in the path to demand stations, for the radial development of the Métro and the SNCF from the Paris center had deprived the region of lateral transportation (see Map 2.4). If the *aérotrain* were to make numerous stops, it would lose all the benefits of speed derived from its unique technology. Finally, a line connecting Paris to the airport at high speed would commit the newest and most expensive technology in mass transit to the exclusive use of an élite of air travelers. Premier Jacques Chaban-Delmas found this arrangement ideologically unsatisfactory; moreover, powerful deputies representing areas potentially affected adversely by the *aérotrain's* noise applied pressure on the premier, who eventually vetoed the plan.

The Gare du Nord–Roissy route was eliminated, then, because of high cost (both financial and political) and ideology; the Orly–Roissy route was eliminated, again because of cost and also because of conflict in applying the technology to the interests of communities in the region. Later plans to use the *aérotrain* between Paris and the new towns of Cergy-Pontoise and Marne-La Vallée, to the northwest and the east, were defeated because of cost and anticipated noise. The link between the airports, in the end, has been developed with conventional carriage through the heart of Paris and thus has moved passengers who otherwise would not have entered the city into the very congestion the National Plans had vowed to relieve.

Aéroport de Paris had counted on the *aérotrain*. When the first major obstacles to its development were encountered, the airport authority organized a joint planning committee, including the SNCF and the RATP. In 1971, after two years of meeting, this Groupe du Travail Paris-Nord equivocated on alternative plans and still hoped for the *aérotrain*. However, consideration was now given to the construction of a rail line from the Gare du Nord.

Roissy-Rail was built in a mere eighteen months. Cost was no object, and no cost analysis preceded the decision that it had to be built. The Cabinet gave the line a crisis priority because the imminent opening of the airport was threatened by the absence of adequate access. The speed with which the line was built compounded the cost, over $80 million (at 1971 prices), 20 percent of the entire cost of building the first phase of the airport: $400 million, including the rail line portion within the airport's boundaries.

Roissy-Rail has been the source of considerable embar-

rassment because the station in the airport is far from
the airline terminal and requires bus transfers. Aéroport
de Paris, pointing to its master plan, insists that the station
site was designated as early as 1965 and confirmed by the
Groupe du Travail Paris-Nord in 1967; with the completion of the airport, the rail station would be nestled amid
three or more airline terminals and therefore would serve
the whole airport. In fact, there is no indication on the
1965 master plans for a station location because no conventional rail link was then contemplated and no site designation had been rendered for the *aérotrain;* the Groupe
du Travail Paris-Nord did not exist in 1967, and its first
recommendations, produced in 1971, did not indicate a
location for the terminus of a mass transit system. The rail
station was built "in the countryside" because by the time
Aéroport de Paris conferred with the SNCF the founda-
tion for Terminal I had been laid and it was too late to run
a railroad into or under the building. Few passengers are
willing to bus to the railroad and then change transportation modes again at Gare du Nord; Roissy-Rail, operating
frequently to maintain scheduling credibility, has been losing upwards of $13,000 per day for lack of traffic since
1976.

Over the long term, the rail station may indeed emerge
in the center of airport activity. However, early plans for
five terminal buildings have disappeared, with the mod-
ules of Terminal II now labeled II–V; the airport was in
operation nearly a decade before even the first module of
Terminal II opened (a full decade later than the date by
which saturation was predicted to occur at Orly and five
years later than the original construction deadline), and it
is unlikely that a third terminal (separate from the module
and originally sited due north) will ever be built. Without
the other terminals, and without the continuation of the
rail line north of the airport (a step that is vaguely contemplated by Paris regional planners), Roissy-Rail is likely to
remain a miniature white elephant, its grand station stand-

ing strangely alone and underutilized on the Plains of France.

Flaws in design: unhappy customers

France's prime minister, Pierre Messmer, personally opened Charles de Gaulle Airport (renamed from Roissy shortly after the president's death) in 1974, two years after the date by which French planners had predicted full saturation at Orly and Le Bourget. Despite some disruption caused by Corsican nationalists, the event was endowed with pomp worthy of a presidential inauguration. The airport was billed as a symbol of French creativity, imagination, prestige, and national unity. It would become, its promoters vowed, the busiest airport for passengers and cargo in continental Europe (they thus carefully excluded London's Heathrow), the envy of airport operators everywhere.

The airport was not ready for a 1972 opening, but it did not matter. Whereas the prediction had indicated excess traffic demand from Orly that Charles de Gaulle would have to absorb, instead assignments had to be transferred from Orly in order to create traffic for the new facility. By the end of 1974, after this transfer, Orly and Charles de Gaulle each operated at about 60 percent of capacity, with the latter only in Phase I of development. Le Bourget's traffic, at the same time, was cut in half. Paris now boasted three seriously underutilized international airports, with more construction in progress – ahead of demand for at least a decade.

The casual traveler, sped along moving ramps, with baggage transferred by computerized robots underground, may be dazzled by the uniqueness of Charles de Gaulle Airport. Terminal I projects futurism and gadgetry unknown in any other airport. But to many airlines, the terminal is too clever and too expensive.

Terminal I imposes an unusual financial burden on airlines because the satellite system requires personnel in at least two completely separate locations. For short-haul carriers like Air Inter, who operated connecting flights for the intercontinental and international traffic out of Terminal I until Terminal II was opened eight years later, ground time circling the one-way terminal was more than double the ground time at Orly. With the move to Terminal II, convenient connections exist exclusively for Air France passengers. Rents are high, in part, the airlines claim, because of design error. Baggage, for example, must be moved up six stories on arrival, a process that requires great and costly energy. The electricity bills for the moving ramps and rechargeable robots continually grow, and when power fails the movements of people and goods are a nightmare. Standing areas are inadequate for the arrival of fully loaded wide-body jets, and the crowding generates chaos at the immigration queues. Worst of all, the circular design contradicts the cardinal rule of flexible construction, for it does not permit expansion: The terminal can never be developed.

Air France was especially unhappy about sharing facilities and baggage handling at Terminal I for over six years. The first module of Terminal II is exclusively Air France's domain, and Runway 2 is destined to serve only Air France and cargo flights. Yet when Terminal II opened, Air France was again miles from the engine-testing zone. Furthermore, Air Force and Aéroport de Paris were in daily negotiations for more than three years, quarreling over the design and management arrangements for the new terminal.

Air Inter and UTA, France's other major airlines, have complained publicly about the airport, particularly with respect to the distribution of traffic between Charles de Gaulle and Orly.[16] Both have foreseen substantial losses, and neither has been eager to open full-scale operations. Union des Transport Aériens (UTA) managed to delay departure from Le Bourget and postpone completion of its module in Terminal II so that it could delay paying

Charles de Gaulle's higher rents. Air Inter opted to maintain most of its operations at the new terminal at Orly, which it regards as ideal; some airlines, including Royal Dutch Airlines (KLM), would also have preferred the new Orly Ouest terminal to assignment at Charles de Gaulle and have been privately jealous of Air Inter.

Air France complains most about the costs associated with operating from two bases in the same metropolitan area. Not even New York City, the greatest air-traveling metropolitan area in the world, generates enough traffic to maintain multiple autonomous facilities that are wholly independent of interairport transfers. Yet Aéroport de Paris maintains that eventually Orly will serve the southern Paris market and Charles de Gaulle the northern Paris market, and each will generate enough traffic to operate independently. In the interim, Air France claims that it is losing passengers who are overflying Paris to avoid the arduous and costly transfer through the city.[17] Although the Ministry of Transport recommended against it, the Cabinet in 1976 voted Air France a special subsidy to offset the costs of moving to Charles de Gaulle and operating at two facilities.

UTA President Antoine Veil complains as much about the principle as about the practicalities of divided traffic.[18] His airline operates from one base, but he notes that Aéroport de Paris has offered no rationale for assignments. In rational France, the distribution of air traffic between Orly and Charles de Gaulle is both illogical and irrational; participation in decisions over distribution, even with the most concerned parties – the airlines – was minimal. And Aéroport de Paris never indicated publicly a rationale for solving the distribution problem.[19]

PARTICIPATION AND CONSULTATION

With the endorsement of the Cabinet, the flexibility of an autonomous budget, the coordination appropriate to narrow purpose, and the promise of monumentalism and national prestige, Aéroport de Paris was able to plan and start to build Charles de Gaulle Airport with virtually no opposition. Landowners, usually the first to challenge airport projects, were bought off. The political Left, lured by the prospect of jobs and economic growth, followed convention and endorsed large-scale public works. Airlines depended on Air France to voice objections, but the state airline was handicapped in a debate against a state agency already enjoying Cabinet approval for its project; moreover, Air France's director when the new airport was being planned assumed that his airline would remain at Orly. The only serious potential for opposition came from the airport's neighbors. They also constituted the only interested party for whom the airport promised no benefits and high costs. They, like the various concerned agencies, were not invited to participate in decision making.

Inhabitants of the communities north of Paris had long been unhappy with Le Bourget, and their pressure contributed to Gibel's initiative in 1957. They opposed Paris-Nord from the moment plans for the site were leaked in 1959, and they formed organizations in each of nine communities, with a central committee to coordinate petitions, demonstrations, and letters to responsible authorities. In 1965 the Gaullist mayor of Roissy-en-France lost to a candidate with no political affiliation – only an identification as an extreme leftist who opposed Communist support for the airport. To counteract Aéroport de Paris's friendly newsletter circulated in the area, entitled *Entre Voisins*, the central citizens' committee published a mocking newsletter identifying themselves more accurately as *Entre Riverains*.

A virtual conspiracy worked against community antagonists. France's national media ignored them, and government officials belittled them as a fractious minority. The airport authority deposited projected noise curves at the Prefecture in order to limit the issuance of building permits near the airport's lands, but managed to keep the curves secret (occasionally even denying their existence after they were on file) so that the communities nearby, and especially in the affluent Vallée de Montmorency, would remain ignorant of the serious impact the airport would have on them. Elected deputies from the area remained silent in Parliament until construction was under way (ten years after the initial plans and nearly four years after public announcement).

Airport opponents did not, moreover, present a united front. Some communities objected to the airport because they wanted to maintain a quiet rural life; others, to the contrary, objected to the airport because it would restrict their industrial growth by limiting building permits. This conflict was particularly acute between the leftist mayor of Roissy-en-France and the traditional Communist mayor of Goussainville. Still others welcomed the airport if it would direct jobs and income to them, but they wanted assurances that urban sprawl and nuisances associated with the airport would not extend to them. This opposition, already divided within, was easy to conquer.

PRESENT GAIN FOR LATER SACRIFICE

The concept of present sacrifice for future gain is the animating idea behind investment. It is necessary to appreciate, however, the presence of indirect investment. It is not possible to identify all the parties who invested in Charles de Gaulle Airport merely by noting who paid money for land acquisition and construction. All those affected, whether as users or as neighbors, had to invest, even unwillingly, in the new airport. In the distribution of costs and benefits, everyone involved needs to be thought of as an investor.

If we consider investment this way, present sacrifice did not yield obvious future gain. Who sacrificed, and who gained? Aéroport de Paris had to raise money and had to jeopardize financial standing; the investment created financial problems the company expected to overcome with the airport's operation. Some airlines thought the cost to move to the new facility and the higher rents would be offset later by customers' enjoyment of the airport. Construction did bring temporary employment for many workers, and the airport's operation did create new jobs. Finally, the property owners whose lands were expropriated made handsome profits.

No one else foresaw any gain, and few enjoyed any. Some companies have profited from development near the airport, but there has been much less satellite growth than was predicted. The highway system has suffered, as have the millions of travelers who have depended on it. The SNCF has carried a growing deficit for Roissy-Rail, and air passengers have spent more time than before between town and terminal. Picardie has lost greenbelt protection; the National Plans have lost their battle for deconcentration and directed commercial growth. In the calculus of present sacrifice and future gain, it is difficult to confirm that Charles de Gaulle Airport has conformed to the three main objectives of French planning.

More than anyone, Charles de Gaulle's neighbors are unhappy, suffering noise and perceiving a loss in property values. They have learned since the airport opened that the noise curves they had never seen reach much further than they had been led by Aéroport de Paris to believe. On this issue, airport challengers have succeeded in winning attention.

Since the introduction of commercial jet aircraft, neighbors of Orly Airport have complained about noise and have demanded state action in their behalf. According to Aéroport de Paris estimates, however, 70,000 people are affected seriously enough by noise at Orly to warrant their moving, a figure that exceeds all budgetary proposals for useful compensation. In the Roissy-en-France area, the sparse population in the seriously affected zone numbered only 1,700 when the airport opened. The total affected by enough noise to warrant soundproofing in the Orly area, again according to Aéroport de Paris, is some 175,000 people; near Roissy there are only 16,700. Moreover, whereas Orly would be able to operate successfully despite a curfew, Aéroport de Paris strategists were determined not to be frustrated in their goal to overcome Frankfurt's lead in cargo services; they planned to keep Charles de Gaulle open 24 hours per day, 365 days per year. With a long-term objective of making Charles de Gaulle Europe's leading airport for all services, the airport authority recognized the logic of compensating neighbors for noise instead of submitting to a curfew.

The Aéroport de Paris solution was to secure through the Cabinet a special noise tax on passengers using Paris airports. This tax does not affect cargo flights or airlines and does not differentiate among planes making greater or less noise. Revenue is deposited into an account that serves to buy homes or subsidize soundproofing in Zone A (the area of greatest noise) and to soundproof public buildings in Zone B.

The noise fund is managed by the very Aéroport de Paris bureau that was responsible for expropriation, now euphemistically renamed the Office for Help to Airport Neighbors. The bureau's principal activity has been to buy homes (without the compensation for inconvenience and relocation that is offered when homes are taken by expropriation) and to demolish them, thus preventing subsequent compensation demands from new occupants. This policy has been felt especially in Roissy-en-France, the village that was to benefit most and even to spread its name through airport development. Most of the buildings in Roissy-en-France have been torn down, though a few have been spared for serving airport employees. Not even able, in the end, to give the airport its name, the village has been spared the airport's continuous impact by being destroyed.

Airport neighbors have objected to these arrangements. They do not think Aéroport de Paris should be paid (for the bureau is supported out of the funds from the special tax) to dispose of properties they excluded from the original expropriation (which was at the authority's expense) by avoiding an earlier public disclosure of noise curves. They find the compensation insufficient because of the pressure on local infrastructure resulting from the increased traffic on their streets and, contrarily, because of the limitations on their development. Compensation to individuals through the purchase of their homes does not help the villages whose lives are altered radically and whose very existence is threatened. And no incentive, under this scheme, has been created for the reduction of noise. Orly neighbors, meanwhile, have remained incensed that no compensation at all has been allocated to them, even though passengers at Orly also contribute to the compensation fund. Realizing that potential costs to serve the Orly population are incalculable, French authorities have made no plans to adjust policy.

Neighbors of Charles de Gaulle are diminishing in number as their homes are acquired and demolished. By 1980 most of Roissy-en-France had disappeared. Thus once again money – this time not even mostly from French pockets, because the tax is higher for international passengers – has purchased silence and the appearance of an efficient, popular, prestigious national facility.

A FINAL ASSESSMENT

According to the British Airports Authority, which processes more passengers annually than Aéroport de Paris, French capacity designations are almost arbitrary. British officials contend that existing Paris infrastructure at Le Bourget and Orly probably could handle twice the traffic French officials consider possible.[20] Even if British authorities exaggerate, it is notable that Aéroport de Paris has never made public any evidence supporting its capacity calculations, on the grounds that such studies are technical and beyond the comprehension of a lay audience. Nor has it introduced any policy designed to modulate peak crowding of the airport and thereby to improve its capacity over the course of the day. Instead, Aéroport de Paris continues to plan and to develop for ever-greater capacity with little budgetary constraint.

Private enterprise could not have afforded the construction of Charles de Gaulle Airport. Only the state could authorize land acquisition at agricultural prices for conversion to more profitable use through compulsory purchase. Only the state could finance a project of the scope of Charles de Gaulle Airport, the largest single construction project in France since the royal palace at Versailles. Only official oversight in the French tradition of the *tutelle* could have guaranteed such planning abuse.[21] And perhaps only the state could cover error with rational argument by purging from the official record a tale of miscalculation and deception reaching as deeply as this one does into the public accounts.

3

The imperial white elephant hunt

The traditional interpretations of French and British post-war performance have emphasized the outcomes of policy choices. French and British decision makers resolved at approximately the same time to build third international airports for their capital cities. The French accomplishment of this objective and the British failure have been cited as examples confirming the more general assessment of effective French central planning and weak British government.

Analysis of the French experience necessarily focuses on the quality of achievement. Given construction, was Charles de Gaulle Airport in fact the product of coherent, coordinated, rational central planning? Was it based on reliable forecasts of air traffic generated by experts with decision-making authority? Did it induce economic growth? Did it respond to identifiable expressions of the general will? Is the airport an efficient symbol of high technological achievement?

A detailed examination of the planning and policy choices for Charles de Gaulle Airport has revealed negative answers to all these questions. These same questions, however, cannot be asked usefully about the third London airport. The airport has not been built, and it is therefore impossible to assess the quality of a facility or a process concluding with its accomplishment. It is possible, nevertheless, to examine the process that yielded a different outcome.

Obviously the analytical task in the case of London's third international airport is different.[1] Whereas the Paris case can be tested against traditional interpretations of French postwar planning as centralized and rational, the London case must be examined according to the conventional explanations for British failure. In one case it is possible to analyze an outcome of physical construction; in the other questions must focus instead on explanation of the process. Some questions, such as those about forecasting, can be asked in both instances, but one cannot inquire in the British case whether economic growth has been induced or whether the facility's achievement is a legitimate symbol of national accomplishment. The more appropriate inquiry for the British case, then, focuses on questions stimulated by the British stereotype. Why did British planners fail to achieve their objective of building a third international airport for London? Are the reasons for failure in this case consistent with conventional explanations? Did the British fail because they were amateurs lacking the necessary expertise for high technology public works? Did they permit too much participation in the planning process? Did stable institutions and a stable two-party system block innovation?

Whereas the third London airport has not been built, none of the conventional explanations corresponds to the details of the case. As in France, there is a chasm between appearances and realities. There have been acrimonious public hearings, for example, but they have not influenced the policy process as many still imagine. There are many amateurs in the civil service, but they have not been the critical actors in this case. There are entrenched civil servants, but they have not governed decisions at key junctures. And although there is apparent continuity in the civil service, there is still more turbulence, underlying a political turbulence that has gone unrecognized by most students of British politics.

Although there is no official version (in contrast to the case in France), detailed descriptions and polemics recounting chronologically the struggle for a third London international airport are available in abundance. Unlike the secret politics of Charles de Gaulle Airport, the dispute in Great Britain has generally been open to the public and exposed to public controversy. The most casual observer cannot help but notice this fundamental difference in the formulation and implementation of public policy.

The third London airport was at the outset considered essential, both inside and outside Britain, for trade and economic well-being. As an island, Britain has a need for ports, whether sea or air, that is beyond doubt. In the 1960s, when criticism of British economic development was loudest (especially in contrast to the situation among the French, the Germans, and the Italians), demands for the third London airport were also loudest. But the airport was not built, and the controversy that has continued for over two decades has become an obsession for analysts of Britain, who point to the country's tradition-bound inability to mobilize government for planning and national success. The substantial accounts of this case have ratified conventional wisdom about postwar Britain.

The story of Charles de Gaulle Airport reveals a public authority unimpeded in pursuit of its narrow objectives. The British story, by contrast, is replete with reversals of policy and stalemate. A casual observer of these cases could not help but surmise that governments which act authoritatively can formulate and implement their goals and that governments which accept principles of participation may be frustrated in achieving what they think is the public interest. But just as French power was more fragmented than might have been supposed, so British stagnation has been attributable less to participation than to other forces. Again, study of the process must modify interpretations of outcomes.

BASIC ISSUES

The controversy over building a third major international airport for London has been continuous since 1953 and has passed through at least ten distinct phases (summarized in Table 3.1). Committees and commissions have been appointed by various governments, and each has made formal and specific recommendations for airport development. The saga has been reported widely, and although the explanations vary the conclusions are always the same.[2] Repeatedly discussion focused on the same site, Stansted, and by 1982 still no land had been taken, nor ground broken, anywhere.

Why were proposals subjected to so many reviews? Why did discussion revolve around Stansted? Why were the recommendations of apparently exhaustive public inquiries rejected repeatedly by governments?

All the available published accounts of the third London airport controversy reach one of two conclusions. One group of analysts is persuaded that, in the end, decisions were made on their merits and government proposals were shown to be inadequately prepared, improperly conceived, and incongruous to implement.[3] A second group believes that citizen activists successfully held government foolishness at bay, probably because of the merits, but certainly because of muscle.[4]

These competing explanations assume that either British planners are incompetent or public participation in Britain paralyzes the execution of public policy. There is a third plausible explanation, however, that depends on neither assumption. Constant changes in government policy have been the result of two entirely different factors: the oscillation of power between the Conservative and Labour parties and the radical reorganizations of government as-

Table 3.1. *Phases of London's third airport plans*

Dates	Party	Starting event	Closing event
1953–60	Conservative	Cmnd. 8902	Reappraisal of traffic growth
1960–3	Conservative	Interdepartmental committee	Report favoring development of Stansted
1964–6	Labour	Inspector appointed	Chelmsford Inquiry emphasizing disadvantages of Stansted
1966–7	Labour	Inspector's report; internal review	Cmnd. 3259 favoring Stansted
1967–8	Labour	Repudiation of Cmnd. 3259	Appointment of Roskill Commission
1969–70	Labour Conservative	Short list of four sites	Publication of Roskill report
1970–1	Conservative	Rejection of Roskill recommendation of Cublington	Proposal of Foulness (near Maplin Sands)
1972–4	Conservative Labour	Establishment of Maplin Development Authority	Termination of Maplin
1974–8	Labour	New interdepartmental study	Cmnd. 7084
1979–	Conservative	Choice of Stansted for development	

sociated with that oscillation. These changes have shifted the responsibility and governing criteria for projects and programs, denuding objectives of necessary continuity and coherent support.

Conventional wisdom

The struggle over the third London airport is understood commonly to involve two sets of actors only, bureaucrats and citizen protesters. Other groups may have participated occasionally (the airlines, experts, politicians), but the two decades of stalemate are said to have resulted either from stubborn and stupid officials facing enlightened citizens or from wise and persistent bureaucrats battling selfish and well-heeled protesters.

The issues involved in the decision to develop additional air facilities and in the selection of a suitable site have been sufficiently polarized to reduce all available interpretations to a simplistic standoff. This analysis is consistent with other examples of British difficulties, especially in the confrontations of industry and labor. Hence published accounts of each stage, focusing on the contest for particular sites (Stansted, Cublington, Maplin Sands), have lauded the intelligence and cunning of citizens while criticizing an overreaching government of faceless bureaucrats; government white papers and documents have insisted upon careful studies leading to inescapable conclusions. The two sides have then assessed all their disagreements within this framework.

Both sides have concurred about the necessity for additional facilities. Government officials forecast a steady traffic growth, and the parties agreed at the outset on three premises defining a response: (1) London must be a "World Air Transport Centre" rivaling New York, so that the United Kingdom will retain its "leading position on world air routes";[5] (2) the United Kingdom, as an industrialized state dependent on overseas trade, requires airports that service trade and earn foreign currency; and (3) demand for air travel should be met by government as a public good.

Consensus on the value of an efficient airport system made consensus for development the inevitable response to a growth in demand. Disagreement arose over where development should take place. The focus on Stansted was, according to government officials, the product of careful analysis that repeatedly demonstrated the site's merits. Amenity groups objecting to development at Stansted argued that the site was preferred because much work was already done. They claimed that the existence of a runway did not of itself justify the construction of another or the broad development of facilities at the site, and they accused the government of laziness and obstinacy in the contrary logic. All seem now to agree that the succession of reviews and studies was the product of citizen protest embarrassing governments and forcing repeated examinations of the same problem. Perhaps more than in any other country, in Britain citizen protest is credited with a dramatic and sustained impact.

A reassessment

As in most disputes, there is some truth on both sides. In many celebrated instances, citizen activists were rich, well connected, and unstintingly selfish. Government bureaucrats frequently were stubborn, illogical, and in some publicly conspicuous cases hysterically zealous over developing civil aviation. And yet there were active citizens concerned honestly for the preservation of the environment, just as there were government officials committed sincerely to the protection of Britain's trade balances. An interpretation that relies on the reports of these two sides necessarily misses much of what happened.

The antagonists understood the significance of political change. Although officials involved in the various plans now tend to minimize the importance of political power oscillating between Conservatives and Labour (thus arrogating to themselves a greater role as the political system's most continuous elements),[6] reverses in policy did correspond to this oscillation, and not by mere coincidence.

Differences between the two political parties that came to power during the twenty years of debate are notable in two respects, policy and political structure. Policies diverged modestly because the premises shared by bureaucrats and citizen groups regarding the need for facilities were accepted by both parties. Nevertheless, Conservative planning in the Heath Government leaned toward grandiose schemes, whereas the first Labour Government of Harold Wilson (1964–6) and his last (1974) shied away from large public works projects. Ironically, the Heath Conservatives had greater faith in government in the arena of public works, and the two parties expressed attitudes toward the organization of government in accordance with their different views on government's role.

The policy differences need amplification, if only to set aside two common arguments. Party leaders tend to emphasize differences, and bureaucrats insist upon continuity in policy despite political changes. Neither argument is entirely correct. Despite the inclination of Labour to propose incremental development, the 1967 white paper (Cmnd. 3259) offered a radical design, expanding Stansted from one runway to four parallel runways, a step that would have given Stansted more operating capacity than any airport in the world. Such development, allegedly for the purpose of absorbing excess traffic from Heathrow and Gatwick, obviously contradicted earlier Labour intentions.

Thus Labour, too, was guilty of planning on a scale remote from medium-term requirements. The Conservatives, by contrast, commonly have argued for the reduction of government activity and the expansion of the private sector. Encouragement of development at Stansted was, when initially proposed by the Conservatives, a modest response utilizing facilities already in place. Yet the Maplin Sands project – planned development of a coastal airport site – demonstrates the Conservative faith in government's capacity and responsibility for managing large capital-intensive efforts that Labour at that time would not have been prepared to contemplate.

The first argument, then, that there are great differences between the parties, must be understood as a valid generalization whose exceptions are not insignificant. There are also important differences within parties that manifest themselves when power shifts internally, as between Wilson and Anthony Wedgwood Benn or between Sir Alec Douglas-Home and Edward Heath. Furthermore, the converse of this generalization, that bureaucrats provide continuity and moderate party differences, appears less accurate.

The role of politics. The Labour Governments of Harold Wilson and James Callaghan believed in government departments with discrete, well-defined tasks. Overlapping policy responsibilities were pursued through interdepartmental committees, usually of civil servants. In some areas, however, Labour was keen to develop governmental efficiency, often by hiving off functions to state enterprises. The British Airports Authority (BAA), for example, was created by Labour in 1965 in order to coordinate the major national air traffic centers and to give a greater business orientation to operations than had been provided by the minister of aviation. Labour began to divide the functions of the Ministry of Aviation, eventually subduing the ministry entirely by transferring its offices to other parts of government. Airports, previously in Aviation, went to a public authority answerable to the president of the Board of Trade.

Whereas Labour was inclined to break down large ministries, the Conservative Government of Edward Heath built them up. Heath believed in "super-ministries" that would consolidate different responsibilities under a single governing roof. Trade, for example, joined Industry, and Environment applied the most comprehensive approach to environmental problems anywhere in the Western world, joining together Transport, Housing and Local Government, and Public Buildings and Works.[7] Under its umbrella came the Maplin Development Authority. When the Conservatives consolidated agencies, they did not necessarily restore functions to the positions they had occupied before Labour separated them. The Ministry of Aviation, for example, was not resurrected, and the third London airport project that had begun there and had been moved to Trade found itself in Environment, with its own public authority created by a separate act of Parliament. Changes in government, then, meant changes in government organization and transfers of responsibility for specific activities from one agency to another (see Fig. 3.1).

The role of bureaucrats. Labour's decision to break down the functions of the Ministry of Aviation meant that aviation responsibilities began moving to agencies of government with different perspectives and objectives. The development of civil aviation was an uncontested public good, in part because the British perceived themselves an island nation dependent on the highest technologies of transportation in order to guarantee trade and a favorable balance of payments. More important, however, ministerial interests were the same as the interests of the aviation industry.

When the Board of Trade assumed more responsibility for airport operations, it scrutinized the balance sheet more than the technology. Economists took seats alongside engineers. The shift was gradual because many of the first officials in Trade overseeing civil aviation came directly from the old ministry or from the national airlines. Nevertheless, criteria were introduced for the assessment of projects that did not imply automatic approval, and different actors began to exercise judgment. Labour's attitude toward government organization encouraged these new considerations.

The Conservative style of government imposed even more radical change. An overseeing minister or an undersecretary carrying multiple responsibilities had to weigh the priorities of civil aviation against competing interests. The Maplin Development Authority, for example, learned quickly from the Transport portfolio in Environment that access to the site would likely prove prohibitive both in cost and in disruption of the countryside, a lesson not learned by the narrower Aéroport de Paris.

Bureaucrats obviously did not guarantee continuity in British politics. Although there is probably less rotation

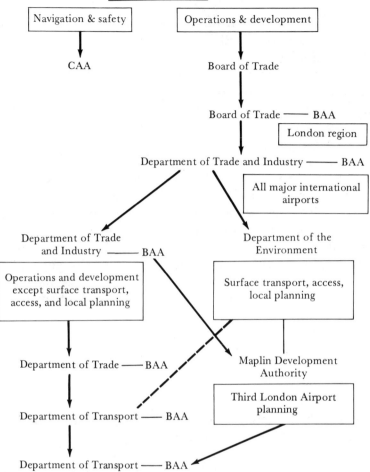

Ministry of Aviation

Navigation & safety   Operations & development

CAA   Board of Trade

Board of Trade ——— BAA
London region

Department of Trade and Industry ——— BAA
All major international airports

Department of Trade   Department of the
and Industry ——— BAA   Environment

Operations and development   Surface transport, access,
except surface transport,   local planning
access, and local planning

Department of Trade ——BAA   Maplin Development
                                   Authority

                                   Third London Airport
                                   planning
Department of Transport ——— BAA

Department of Transport ——— BAA

Key
——————▶ Devolution of authority
——————— Tutelle
– – – – Subordinate
▢ Functions

Figure 3.1. Transfers of responsibility from the Ministry of Aviation.

among jobs in Britain than in some other parliamentary systems (such as Canada's), British civil servants generally do not stay entrenched in particular responsibilities over the decades involved in major projects. Certainly British civil servants are no more entrenched than the French, against whom this criticism, for planning at least, is not leveled. The "departmental view" may have a life of its own, but responsibility for projects shifts with government reorganization, and such reorganization is even more frequent than exchanges of power between the two major parties because of conceptual differences (and personal power struggles) within the parties themselves. However resistant or resilient this view may be, the criteria of ministerial responsibility eventually prevail – unless supplanted by the different criteria of a still different ministry. For these reasons, British government is remarkably unstable, and long-term projects are exceedingly difficult to accomplish.

THE THIRD LONDON AIRPORT CASE

Stansted

The 1953 white paper (Cmnd. 8902) proposed rationalization of London's airport system to cope with an anticipated doubling of scheduled flights during the next decade, through the designation of a single main international depot (Heathrow) with a principal backup and a third facility in reserve. The seven airports operating in the region threatened coherent air traffic control. A public inquiry the next year helped establish Gatwick as London's second airport. The third was not yet identified.

By the late 1950s London enjoyed the status of Europe's leading air transportation center, but traffic growth marked by an increase in traffic movements exceeding the 1953 predictions seemed to threaten the area's runway and air traffic control capacities. Neighbors of London's second airport, Gatwick, were hostile to traffic growth south of the Thames. Runway expansion at Heathrow generally was precluded and other development restricted by a combination of design and location: The airport's Star of David design closed in the terminals (see Map 3.1); London's sewage works prevented major construction outside the airport's boundaries west and south; and there was a motorway to the north and conurbation north and east. A consensual commitment to maintain London's preeminence in civil aviation combined with political and physical obstacles at the two main facilities in the region to encourage new growth where traffic in the past had been minimal.

The London Airport Development Committee predicted in 1957 that traffic would exceed Heathrow's capacities in 1970;[8] the committee urged further development of Gatwick and possible recourse to a third airport. Three years later, the Estimates Committee of the House of Commons demanded immediate investigation into Stansted's suitability for London's third airport, expressing skepticism about the site and concern about development in the region.[9] The minister of aviation subsequently appointed a committee according to the recommendation of the Estimates Committee, one dominated by airline representatives, members of government departments committed to airport development, and spokesmen of the National Air Traffic Control Services. This interdepartmental committee, chaired by George Hole, convened in November 1961 and published its recommendation for the development of Stansted as London's third airport in 1964.

Pressure to focus on Stansted had begun innocently. The site boasted the longest extendable (to twelve thousand feet) runway in Britain, built for military purposes and abandoned by the Americans. The Hole Committee argued that Stansted was the most inexpensive, accessible solution to London's air traffic problems and set down criteria that governed thinking for the next two decades. Stansted's air

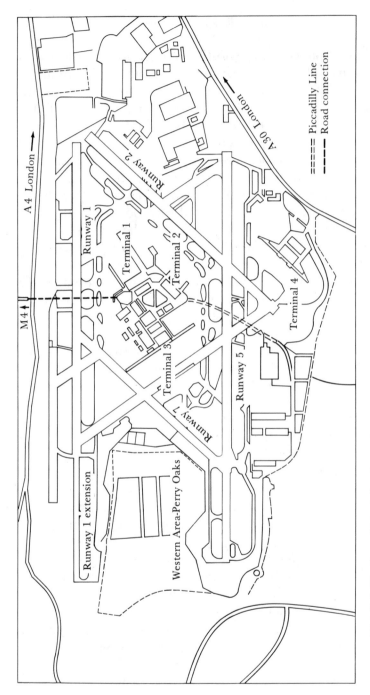

Map 3.1. Heathrow Airport, London.

routes could be independent of Heathrow and Gatwick because the latter were west and south of the city, whereas Stansted lay to the north. Transportation from Stansted to central London, on existing roads, took less than one hour (although the 1953 study was critical of surface access, and the problem would plague later deliberations); the land was already committed to civil aviation and more land would not be needed; there was a nearby labor force (Bishop's Stortford, with eighteen thousand people); meteorological difficulties were minimal; and military air bases were distant and posed no conflict. Only additional terminal facilities and extremely modest air traffic control capacities would be necessary to upgrade Stansted for the proposed use.

The plans were limited but demanded immediate response: The committee predicted runway saturation for Heathrow and Gatwick within a decade. Despite the modesty and urgency of the proposal, however, it fell victim to two forces. Wealthy and powerful neighbors opposed any development in this, Chancellor of the Exchequer R. A. Butler's, constituency. When they learned that the Hole Committee visited only the Stansted site while claiming consideration of more than one hundred locations, they launched a vigorous objection that helped delay the planning process.[10]

The interdepartmental review did not expect to implement change quickly despite the appeal for prompt action. Planning was well in advance of need. With the upgrading, Stansted would be able to absorb excess traffic until the late 1960s, so there was time to wait for protest to subside. Release of the final report was delayed nine months until March 1964, but by that time more actors had become concerned with development plans, and more attention was being paid to the long term.

Despite the committee chairman's inclination merely to upgrade the use of Stansted's single runway (allowing for possible future development of a second runway),[11] the committee declared a need for two additional runways in the London area that could be spaced sufficiently to permit simultaneous operations and that could accommodate supersonic airliners. The recommendation eliminated the Gatwick option, where only one additional runway could be built. It also triggered local protest again at Stansted, and it worried the national airlines, British Overseas Airways Corporation (BOAC) and British European Airlines (BEA), neither of which wanted to move any operations from Heathrow.

The criteria for site selection, constant throughout the search, made Stansted a likely if not inevitable choice. Nowhere else within an hour of London was there a substantial operational runway available to commercial aircraft. But Ministry of Aviation planners escalated their demands for land and runways, a tactic that more than any other single factor delayed development and encouraged the study of other sites. If more than one runway were essential, then Stansted's relative advantage would decline with increases in perceived construction requirements. The relationship of a multiple runway system to London's air traffic patterns would demand realignment, effectively sacrificing the runway already in place. And more construction and more land meant more money, which worried government; more traffic, which worried neighbors; and more dispersed operations, which worried airlines.

Consultations with local authorities began shortly after release of the report prepared for a Conservative Government. So did the tenure of a Labour Government, which promised a public inquiry. Nevertheless, the new minister of aviation repeated his predecessor's dictum that the need for facilities and the timing of their construction were technical issues outside the purview of the inspector named by the Ministry of Housing and Local Government to conduct a new inquiry specifically into Stansted. National policy, the minister of aviation said in a press conference, could not be subjected to a local inquiry that was convened for "human considerations."

The new inquiry conducted at Chelmsford, generated by a change in Government, did not begin until December 1965; it was completed in February 1966 and the inspector's report was ready in June, though it was withheld eleven months.[12] Revealing renewed doubt about Stansted, it was released with the Labour Government's White Paper on Airports Policy, which criticized and rejected the report.

Delays were the product of internal government review and reorganization. Julian Amery, the Conservative minister of aviation, had passed on to Roy Jenkins, Labour minister of aviation, a proposal that had escalated from the immediate adaptation of existing facilities to substantial new construction; Jenkins's Government redistributed the functions of his ministry, and the new report prepared at his request was delivered to Douglas Jay, president of the Board of Trade. Jay inherited a white paper that had been prepared on the basis of assumptions from the Ministry of Aviation in the Conservative Government, and by the time it went through his office, the only continuity in its preparation resided with zealous aviation enthusiasts, especially Peter Masefield (former chairman of BEA and chairman of Labour's BAA, established in 1965), who constantly fueled the plans with greater infrastructure demands. The one additional runway had become two and then four, and the government had to impose a three-line whip in June 1967 to defend an airports policy it did not seem to understand.[13]

Economists inside the Board of Trade began examining the proposal for the first time in June, after it had been presented to the House of Commons. Although it lay within their jurisdiction, in the transition from the Ministry of Aviation it had escaped their scrutiny. They told Jay that the report supporting the white paper lacked all methodological respectability. Forecasts developed strictly by statisticians took no account of economic forces, and reasonable social concerns differentiating sites in the London area had been ignored altogether. Jay gave them a month to offer an alternative, and they reported in July their preference for Nuthampstead, a different site. By then, Jay had resigned.

The new president of the Board of Trade, Antony Crosland, invited further internal study. The subject, and the portfolio, were new to him, but he understood the narrowness of the Ministry of Aviation's preparations. Only one member (of sixteen) of the initial interdepartmental study did not represent an aviation interest;[14] the study for the 1967 white paper had no representation from outside the ministry at all. Crosland gave new emphasis to Housing and Planning and required all further investigation to be expressly interdepartmental.

Goodbye Stansted − for now. The Stansted Development Order from the white paper was legally flawed because the call for a realignment of Stansted's runway would require a public hearing.[15] Avoidance of a public hearing on what he had thought an indefensible proposal was an additional incentive for Crosland to reconsider the plans.

Crosland took the new findings for Nuthampstead to the Cabinet, where he found resistance to the repudiation of a Government white paper. However, there was strong opposition to Stansted in the House of Lords, stimulated by the personal interests of certain members. Labour, committed to reform of the Upper Chamber, permitted this mission to take precedence over the matter of the airport site. Crosland finessed the withdrawal of Stansted in consideration of the Government's priorities and with the threat of a public hearing owing to the runway realignment. Stansted, temporarily, was out of consideration.[16]

There can be no doubt that the presence of organized opposition to Stansted influenced Labour's thinking. However, the review of the site was the product of government reorganization and the concerns of new actors, chiefly economists in the Board of Trade. The responsible minister, new to the controversy, was persuaded by his civil servants and fearful of embarrassment at public hearings over a proposal that he did not develop.

The Roskill Commission

The persistent assumption supporting a search for London's third international airport derived from three circumstances. First, the BAA was mandated to "provide such services and facilities as are in its opinion necessary or desirable" at the aerodromes within its authority: Heathrow, Gatwick, Stansted, and Prestwick.[17] Priority for appointment as BAA members was to be given to "persons who appear to the Minister to have had wide experience of and to have shown capacity in air transport," a stipulation which assured that perceptions of necessary facilities would follow the interests of the air industry.[18]

The second assumption emerged from the first. Although the BAA had authority to acquire other airports, the authentic third airport in the London area, Luton, belonged to Luton Borough Council, which had no interest in selling. Luton drew most of London's charter traffic, carrying more than four times the number of passengers, nearly 650,000 in 1968, that was going through Stansted. Indeed, in 1967 the BAA projected that Luton might carry as many as 2 million passengers in the 1980s; by 1971, Luton already handled 2.7 million, compared to Stansted's 474,000. Yet discussion of a third airport systematically ignored Luton. Owing to a large population nearby and to the topography, a second runway was considered impractical, and the facility's growth potential was therefore circumscribed. The BAA did not control the airport and stubbornly thought it inappropriate for projected needs. While Luton performed the function projected for Stansted, the BAA dreamed still of an airport to rival Heathrow.

The third assumption derived from traffic forecasts. As in no other country, experts in Britain utilized forecasts to help shape rather than merely justify policy. But British forecasters proved no more skilled than their counterparts elsewhere. They, too, overestimated growth and underestimated capacity and improved air traffic control.

With traffic in BAA airports concentrated at Heathrow and Gatwick, the BAA could develop Stansted or seek a whole new facility. There was no wavering from the main mission, "the selection of a site for a Third London Airport acceptable to the travelling public and to the airlines which will use it," a mission "essential to the task of maintaining London's position as the World's largest centre of international travel."[19] The authority refused to contemplate alternative strategies for adjusting the market demand because they implied a reduction in the quality of service. Many pages were written warning of the construction of Paris's new airport at Roissy-en-France, which "will clearly be in competition with London for international traffic."[20] If Paris offered the use of facilities without restrictions, the BAA warned, international travelers would prefer Paris to London.

Crosland's reluctance about Stansted led to a systematic search for a new site, not to the abandonment of costly development. In February 1968 he formally repudiated Stansted by announcing a new inquiry, and in May the Roskill Commission (named for the judge who served as its chairman) was appointed "to inquire into the timing of the need for a four runway airport to cater to the growth of traffic at existing airports serving the London area, to consider the various alternative sites, and to recommend which site should be selected."[21] An examination of timing allowed for delay, but the appointment of the commission assumed an eventual need for four additional runways in the London area. Hence, the terms of the ultimate aviation demand in the early 1960s defined the agenda for the 1970s.

Science and politics. The report of the Roskill Commission surely is one of the most celebrated, and least understood, of all government studies.[22] Costing some £2 million and producing thirteen published volumes, the commission applied the most advanced and sophisticated techniques of cost–benefit analysis to recommend the single best site for a third international airport serving the London region. Public hearings were held and a full range of views was solicited before the report was issued.

There are three main points to be made about the Roskill Commission as an episode in the saga of London's airport development, and each contradicts conventional wisdom about the commission itself and about British planning in general. First, the commissioners, not the expert research staff, pressured for a virtually unlimited application of cost–benefit techniques. Second, the short list of sites was not a set of recommendations, not a priority list, nor even a list of wholly acceptable sites. Third, the Conservative Government that received the report certainly did not understand its contents and very likely did not even read it.

These points are essential for three reasons: (1) Roskill frequently is cited as an example of Britain's incompetence in planning, yet political forces, not the planners or researchers, undermined the deliberate inquiry; (2) the failure to study or understand the report has led to widespread ridicule of its contents; and (3) the commission was appointed by a Labour Government but reported to a Conservative Government that had visions of grandiose development not promised by the commission's recommendations.

The commission invited testimony that might have challenged the premise of building a new airport for London, but neither the need nor the value was ever questioned by witnesses.[23] The criticism of the mandated assumption came only with the commission's published report. The greatest objections were reserved, however, for the shortlisting. Here were expressed two main concerns. First, Stansted was not on the final list of sites. This affront to previous analysts caused political damage that robbed the commission of potential defenders, especially among those who shared objections to a coastal site. Second, the commission did include a coastal site, thereby apparently endorsing the possibility of construction well away from the conurbation.

Both these concerns arose from the shortlisting technique, the process through which countless conceivable sites were reduced to four feasible or desirable locations. As part of the technique, the research team employed a process of elimination, comparing sites in pairs within specified categories. For example, Foulness and Shoeburyness were compared within the category of coastal sites, with the latter eliminated by the Ministry of Defence because of an artillery range. A pair was compared and the better site (according to the cost–benefit criteria) survived in order to be compared with a third site, always within a specific category. Theoretically, Stansted could have been the third best site in England and still not have appeared on this short list because within its category the commission opted, ironically, for Nuthampstead, the very site favored in Trade's internal study, whose results were unknown to the Roskill Commission. Moreover, the coastal site might not have ranked among the first hundred sites in England, for its inclusion was the result of a desire to meet a perceived public demand for some alternative to the inland sites. The research team believed the case for Foulness so obviously weak that commitment to an inland site would be reinforced by its inclusion.

Whatever the merits to be found in the analytical sophistication of the research team (and they certainly are debatable), they were offset by political naïveté. Interested parties who had argued for years that Stansted was the inevitable site were unable to believe that it was not listed among final possibilities; promoters of a coastal site insisted that the commission had endorsed such a choice. Hence inland site advocates rejected the commission because of Stansted's total exclusion, and coastal site defenders embraced the commission only by repudiating the principal recommended site. Wary of the crudeness of the cost–benefit techniques, the research team recommended one site – Cublington – but declined to rank order the other three choices on the short list. This decision to defend intellectual integrity, including the rejection of a more politically defensible site – Thurleigh – exacted incalculable political cost, for it suggested that the three other sites, including Foulness on the coast, were equivalent. The commission never regarded Foulness as a serious possibility (indeed, Foulness was systematically rejected in both its two- and its four-runway configurations, Colin Buchanan's public dissent notwithstanding),[24] but commissions are expected to remain silent after reporting, and the public failure to grasp the technique frustrated the staff without producing clarification.

The announcement of four sites (see Map 3.2) on a short list preceded publication of the commission's report recommending Cublington and thereby encouraged public protest at each site. Such movements stirred public comment and attention but had no palpable effect on the Government decision to accept the report but reject its recommendation. Had there been such direct influence, the Government might have displayed greater awareness of the contents of the report.

John Davies, the minister of trade and industry who received the Roskill Report (commissioned by the president of the Board of Trade), believed that Foulness was "one of a series of possible sites" and knew nothing of the short-listing techniques. He defended the rejection of Cublington on both "political" and "environmental" grounds but made no distinction between the two.[25] Prime Minister Edward Heath's Central Policy Review Staff (CPRS), headed by Lord Rothschild, whose home was near the Cublington

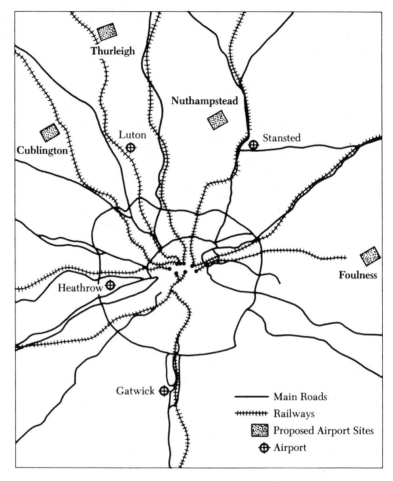

Map 3.2. London area airports and final Roskill Commission sites.
Reprinted by permission of the publisher from Elliot J. Feldman and
Jerome Milch, Technocracy versus Democracy: The Compara-
tive Politics of International Airports *(Boston, Mass.: Auburn*
House Publishing Co., 1982).

site, inveighed analytically against the coastal site but con-
veyed an equivocal recommendation to the Cabinet.[26] The
prime minister was in consultation with the Port of London Authority, which was keen to create a superport on
the coast.[27] With the Stansted option discarded by Roskill,

Table 3.2. *Special studies for the third London airport*

Interdepartmental committee on the Third London Airport (Hole Committee)	1960
Chelmsford Inquiry	1965
Roskill Commission	1968
Maplin Development Authority	1971
Interdepartmental review	1974

Note: These were studies conducted outside the normal business or internal assessments of government departments.

Table 3.3. *Sites chosen for London's third airport*

Stansted (1–2 runways)	1960
Stansted (4 runways)	1967
Cublington	1970
Foulness	1971
Maplin Sands	1971
Stansted (2 runways)	1978

the Cabinet decided to reject Cublington, ignore the shortlisting technique, and opt for the site regarded by Roskill's researchers as by far the least acceptable. Thus was the Maplin Sands project, on a site near Foulness that would be more accommodating for overall superport development, born of political design and expert naïveté; and thus once again the decisions governing the third London airport oscillated in a political wind despite the careful planning of civil servants, expert staff, and commissioners (see Tables 3.2 and 3.3).

Maplin mud

The Roskill Commission reported in December 1970 and saw its Cublington recommendation rejected in Parliament in April 1971. The Government announced plans to develop a coastal site as part of a mammoth superport-airport project to compete at once with Rotterdam by sea and any facility in all of Europe by air. The first runway was promised by 1980. The undertaking, moreover, was considered essential because one government forecast predicted saturation at Heathrow and Gatwick by 1972, whereas another foresaw 1976–7 as the critical juncture. All agreed that more runways were desperately needed by the late 1970s.

Maplin Sands was one of several bold projects on the Conservative agenda. The "chunnel" connecting France and England finally was to be realized after centuries of schemes and discussions. Motorways were to ring London. And Concorde, members of the Government seemed to believe, was to become the front line of Britain's assault on the world's aviation markets. Each project required advanced technology, unprecedented capital investment, and long-term planning. And all were to be accomplished at once.

Economics undercut the feasibility of each project, and none more than Maplin Sands. The Maplin Development Bill of October 23, 1973, acknowledged that the site's selection did not include three critical assessments: of the actual costs for the site, of cost comparisons with other solutions to the airport capacity demands, and of compatibility with regional policies. The Conservative Government, under Section 2 of the bill, ordered a review of the project with a directive for opening the facility in 1982. The Labour Government canceled the review and ordered another that ignored the seaport plans entirely. The review estimated in 1974 that the land acquisition and preparation and the construction of a two-runway airport on the site would cost £400 million. An additional £235 million would be required for access to the remote site.[28]

These costs derived from a £50 million bill for land reclamation, because Maplin is, as its name implies, sand, and for more than £100 million for the relocation of defense facilities at Shoeburyness because of its proximity to the Maplin Sands site. The access costs were derived from distance between the site and London. Because the concept had shifted again, this time downward from four runways, the cost to settle on the coast seemed all the more exorbitant.

The change in calculated need by 1974 resulted from two factors not apparent when the Roskill Commission reported: The jumbo jet pressured terminal capacities but reduced runway demand, and the oil crisis confirmed an overall decline in the rate of traffic growth. Less optimistic forecasts from the BAA moved back the date of predicted saturation at Heathrow and Gatwick more than a decade. Furthermore, whereas the airport may have seemed environmentally acceptable because it was far from people (conforming to the Conservative concept of acceptable impact), the roads and rails to service it would tear through the countryside. Hence Labour decided to defend an environment of Brent geese and unspoiled fields. The costs, however, exceeding £2 billion,[29] clearly constituted the decisive opposition. As the Roskill research team had foreseen, the political plan on sand, after careful study by skilled civil servants, sank into the mud.

AFTERMATH

The Labour Government canceled Maplin within four months of instituting its review. The thirty-man bureaucracy that had grown up as the "Special Third London Airport Directorate" inside the Department of the Environment was dismantled. The most comprehensive multidisciplinary project yet organized in British government outside the prosecution of war (and following the most comprehensive cost–benefit analysis ever undertaken anywhere) was written off at a cost of £2.6 million, a sum that involved planning and no on-site preparation. This expense also excluded planning done by British Rail, the Port of London Authority, and the BAA (for the main terminal design), all of whom were left off the directorate itself.

The Maplin development exercise proved beyond doubt that the British were as capable of comprehensive planning as the French. It also proved they were capable of comparably grandiose visions. But, unlike the French, the British lacked two elements, continuous authority and a willingness to accept luck, in this case the apparent availability of at least one accessible, preexisting runway.

The constant change in British plans commonly has been attributed to citizen protest, but it is clear that changes were internal to government and followed elections and government reorganizations. Citizens did stimulate delays, but mostly through the structures that encouraged their participation. Public hearings over Stansted and for the Roskill Commission plainly extended decision processes. Derrick Wood's environmental campaign against a coastal site surely affected political thinking,[30] but his success was premised on the frustration of the Roskill research team. Their report repudiated by the Conservatives, they were prepared to lobby Labour, and especially Antony Crosland, who had organized the commission, in anticipation of Labour's return to power. Although the regular meetings with Crosland and Wood at St. Stephen's Tavern were outside the apparatus of government, access was a function of changing governments and the appointment of a special commission, both structural conditions generally absent in the French Fifth Republic. It is notable, indeed, that the man who created Roskill as president of the Board of Trade returned to the Cabinet with the Environment portfolio; responsibilities for the third London airport had been transferred there by the Conservatives, and Crosland was given the extraordinary opportunity to reject the rejecters. It is impossible to know or speculate on the outcome had Crosland not been out of office when the Roskill Commission recommended Cublington.

The instability that contributed to these results was not peculiarly British. As we shall see, the French Cabinet frequently is shuffled, and portfolios often are expanded or collapsed. But this kind of instability affected a different political system, with different institutional arrangements, in Britain. Whereas such instability in France could shelter powerful agencies and thus extend their authority, in Britain projects became more exposed to political winds.

No felicitous new site was available to British planners. Unlike the land expanse that by historical accident remained undeveloped and close to Paris, land near London inevitably affected sizable populations and valued buildings. Hence British planners did not have the apparent luck of the French; they were obliged to think either very modestly, in order to limit disruption, or very ambitiously, in order to justify long travel distances and land reclamation. Participation encouraged more serious thought about social costs or alternative plans, but it did not disrupt the planning itself.

Despite these appearances, French luck must not be overstated. One might argue that luck was on the side of the British, for Stansted was already an operating airport with the longest runway in the United Kingdom and reliable access to London. A political, not a technical, decision imposed a requirement for a more substantial tract of land. Hence the choice of scale counted even more heavily in British conflict than the accident of geography.

After the Maplin cancellation the Labour Government ordered comprehensive national and London area airport plans. The planners, removed from the Conservatives' concentration in the Department of the Environment, were centered in the Department of Trade; they produced in February 1978 a white paper that demonstrated, among other things, the absence of an emergency in the accommodation of air travel demand.[31] London survived twenty years without the construction deemed in 1960 to be indispensable, and no evidence surfaced of traffic loss owing to competition with other countries. The Conservative Government that inherited Labour's planning documents proposed returning to Stansted, but foresaw not even a second runway before 1990. The essence of British airport plans into the new century is flexibility and minimum construction.

The present, and probably not final, outcome of London's third airport saga bears witness to planning whose personnel and criteria have kept changing. Plans began in the Ministry of Aviation under a Conservative Government; they then went through an interdepartmental committee dominated by aviation interests, to an independent inspector appointed by the Ministry of Housing and Local Government in a Labour Government, to twin responsibilities in the new BAA and the Board of Trade, through a special commission appointed by Labour that delivered its report to a Conservative Government, to the new Department of the Environment (with some concerns remaining in the BAA, the Civil Aviation Authority, and the newly amalgamated Department of Trade and Industry), and back to the Department of Trade (again under Labour); and finally they were subjected to a new interdepartmental study organized by Trade in cooperation with Environment. All these changes took place between 1961 and 1975, while international economics challenged forecasting optimism and technical change (particularly improved air traffic control and wide-body jets) reduced pressure on runways – the key to perceived requirements for new sites and construction.

CONCLUSION

The prevailing assumption of both Conservative and Labour Governments throughout this process was that the air-traveling public merited policy priority because Britain's island character required competitive port facilities for sea and air. Experts serving both parties forecast a demand that would exceed available facilities, and governments of both parties agreed that Britain's competitive position would be harmed by any restrictions on airport use. The public interest in trade could be served only by the construction of additional aviation facilities.

The assumptions of British experts were the same as the assumptions of their counterparts in France, although French reasoning from these assumptions was not always the same as the British. As the British talked of the commercial requisites of an island nation, the French talked of the obligations of Continental leadership. But whether for profit or prestige, the decision to build new airports was the same. Despite the conventional wisdom that the incentive for French decisions is technocratic and for British political, traffic forecasts inspired British thinking about airport construction; French forecasts were summoned to justify prior political instructions. Nevertheless, both French and British forecasters failed to distinguish themselves: Their degrees of error were similar, whatever the timing of their estimates, for three decades.

The central distinctive feature of the British technical process involved recognition that different experts value different criteria. In France the narrow mandate of Aéroport de Paris was to build and exploit civil aviation infrastructure. The British Ministry of Aviation was assigned a similar mission, but whereas Aéroport de Paris controlled the third Paris airport case from inception to completion, the British ministry was abolished. Responsibility for airport development was held at different times in Britain by engineers, economists, and environmentalists. Whereas French experts involved in the development of Charles de Gaulle Airport were responsible strictly for airports, British experts at various times shared responsibilities for housing, local government, airports, environmental protection, surface transportation, trade balances, and industrial development.

The British assumption of need remained constant, but

priorities continuously wavered. These changes resulted from formal transfers of the airport portfolio, which in turn resulted from formal reorganizations of government. The problem was not merely one of shifting personnel. Rather, it derived from the introduction of different experts with different responsibilities in different agencies and departments. This perpetual government reorganization flowed from the different concepts of government harbored by the Conservative and Labour parties that, for more than three decades, alternated in power. From the first serious discussion of a third international airport in London, no party lasted in power more than six years.

British structures guarantee limited participation. However much public hearings were denounced as sham by disappointed critics, they devoured quantities of time in the life of transitory governments. They circulated criticism of government publicly and encouraged parliamentary debate. They gave reassurance to skeptical civil servants even as they insulted and infuriated more confident ones. Such participation thus was never decisive: No evidence at any juncture – whether in establishing the interdepartmental review, or the Chelmsford Inquiry, or the Roskill Commission, or repudiation of Cublington, or cancellation of Maplin Sands, or any other turning point – supports the assertion that popular participation was essential, or even seriously considered, in decision making. Even in the apparently populist episode in the House of Lords, members' own interests were primary. The many tracts on this subject take on faith the causal relationship between public protest and agreeable public policy. But hearings did sustain an atmosphere of criticism, and they did periodically introduce the delays that permitted projected costs to exhaust estimated resources.

Popular participation, then, was not decisive. Neither was the compromising participation of bargaining élites, for as in France the airport portfolio normally was held closely by experts with a narrow mandate. The French experts, and their mandate, seemed eternal, whereas British experts were able to protect their mandates only briefly. The crucial difference was not the participation of competitors but rather their sequential governance and the brevity of the time during which any one expert group controlled the portfolio.

Such portfolio movement says nothing about British competence. The numerous studies and reports, however, say a great deal. In their thoroughness and sophistication they often far exceeded the quality of the French documents. But they were often conceived narrowly, and when more broadly set (as was Roskill), they were political victims. Indeed, the Roskill experience alone is a precious miniature for the longer story: a report solicited by one party delivered to another, a research team pressured politically to overstep consciously its own expertise, the shifting criteria of responsibility leading to gross reinterpretation of recommendations.

The conventional explanations for British experience are not supported by the third London airport case. Moreover, the more powerful explanation for British failure to build a third London airport contradicts other conventional wisdom. Stable Britain cannot accomplish high technology public works projects because the stability is an illusion and the political standoff of Conservatives and Labour (compounded by their own internal divisions) disrupts whatever continuity or expertise (or both) might have been provided by a once-admired bureaucracy.

4

The albatross

The building of Charles de Gaulle Airport can no more be called a "success" than the nonconstruction of a third international airport for London can be termed a "failure." Aéroport de Paris accomplished its objective of building a technologically sophisticated airport able to absorb all traffic through Paris for the foreseeable future, but it failed to provide adequate access, satisfied clients (the airlines), or contented neighbors. It did not rationalize services with a second Paris international airport, and because it did not do so it may have contributed to a decline in the region's traffic; nor did it stimulate major economic growth. The goal, therefore – that of assuring Paris its place as the premier air facility attraction in Europe – may have been sacrificed to the narrow objective.

These deficiencies resulted because the French made political choices without planning (by determining to build a grand-scale facility before forecasting requirements or studying implications) and because the principal responsible agency enjoyed broad powers of expropriation, fiscal borrowing, and construction but a narrow mandate to build and exploit commercially. Forecasts generated after the political choices had been made were inaccurate, and the agency was at different times both unwilling and unable to cooperate with other government departments. According to the criteria typical of the literature on French planning, and characteristic of self-judgment among French officials in central planning agencies and in the Commissariat Général du Plan,[1] Charles de Gaulle Airport is a failure: It does not resolve Paris's air traffic problems, it compounds surface transit difficulties, it contravenes National Plans. Neither its planning nor its execution was "rational," devoid as both stages were of careful cost–benefit analysis, coordination with implicated clients and agencies, local communities, and individuals.

An objective of British planners was to match the third Paris airport with one for London. Unlike the French, the British did rely on forecasts and planning procedures before reaching a decision to build or choosing a site. No single agency was empowered to build, and a series of interdepartmental committees and studies revealed obstacles to all potential sites and plans. Even as political decisions to build were periodically made, planners identified problems and politicians changed their minds (and even more frequently, changed the planners). To a significant degree, the British applied the French planning ideal. Consequently, after substantial expenditure and continuous public and governmental controversy, the British never acquired land and never built any part of a third London airport.

The goal of responsible British officials – to satisfy air traffic demand through the twentieth century – has been achieved during the quarter century of debate over a new airport. There is no evidence that the absence of a new facility has contributed to any decline in traffic. Clients generally are happy with current arrangements, present neighbors have been pacified, and potential neighbors have been much relieved. No new pressure has been placed on the surface transit system; and indeed, an extension of the Piccadilly underground line to Heathrow Airport has relieved some motorway congestion. Failure in the objective of building a new airport may even have helped achieve the goal of serving the air-traveling public efficiently with minimal disruption to other services.

The Paris process and outcome show France to be more political and less technocratic than commonly supposed. The London process and outcome show the British to be more professional and more oriented toward planning than critics traditionally have charged. British "failure" has been largely in the political insistence upon the objective without careful study of its relationship to overall goals, whereas French failure has lain more directly in the planning procedures. These judgments, however, derive primarily from the stereotypes: Given the expectation that the French will be rational and technocratic, the British amateurish and compromising, these cases reveal considerable unprofessional incoherence for one and professional obstinacy for the other.

If these cases are removed from the expectations created by traditional analyses, then the outcomes set them apart more than the procedures. The French may not have tried to coordinate, but when the British tried (especially in the example of the Maplin Sands directorate) they failed. The French may have begun their planning with prior political choices, but party politics and competing concepts of government intervened continuously in Britain. Both the French and the British displayed a sizable quotient of highly skilled and professional civil servants, and both produced similar estimates of traffic and assessments of need at comparable times. In sum, despite the different outcomes, the cases reveal French and British planning – and political involvement – to be highly similar.

These similarities can be confirmed by observing the parallel experiences of Britain and France in a joint project. Among the many judgments pronounced on Concorde is the view that the British wavered when the French were steadfast. The British constantly wanted to cancel the project, to whittle down its expense, to scale down its vision. The French, it is argued, were more confident, willing to indulge in extravagance so that greatness could be achieved. The British were confined to commerce, the

French were meeting their destiny. The overall image is one of contest more than cooperation, with each country reverting to cultural type.

A detailed review of the Concorde experience reveals again that this traditional view is distorted. Not only did Britain and France overcome the stereotyped expectation that they could not accomplish such a monumental technological task together; they also displayed the same hesitations, and the same vision. Indeed, close scrutiny may even suggest that the British from the outset were more confident and more visionary than the French. Whatever the later styles of advertising and promotion, the substance of the national experiences sustains the portrait of similarity.

In their rhapsody to Concorde, British authors F. G. Clark and Arthur Gibson have written, "In scale and complexity, the Concorde programme is comparable to the U.S.A.'s Apollo Moon-shot programme; as a venture in technological collaboration between two major industrial nations, Concorde is unique."[2] Robert Gilpin called Concorde for France "the functional equivalent of the space and nuclear weapons programs."[3] Such is the official view of Concorde in both Britain and France. Yet the rhapsody has been ridiculed because the plane proved a commercial disaster.

As assessment of Concorde is difficult because interpretations of its success and failure have led to irreconcilable exaggerations. Nevertheless, critics agree on three apparent truths. First, Concorde is a significant technical achievement, "the world's most advanced passenger aircraft," according to the criterion of speed.[4] Second, the collaborators who produced the plane had been thought too different to cooperate on any project, let alone one of such complexity, risk, and expense. Given the assumption that the French were effective long-term planners and the British were not, it seemed unlikely that they could work together for some fifteen years to plan and execute a project. But, third, the plane is a total failure commercially and has set back the aircraft industry in both Britain and France. The two countries proved they could collaborate, but the consequences were not enviable.

These apparently contradictory truths can be reconciled, but only by altering conventional views of Concorde's partners. First, at least in planning and technical development Britain and France are not as dissimilar as commonly supposed. Second, collaboration does not necessarily lead to greater wisdom; two pocketbooks provided more money than one, but the arrangements encouraged expenditure instead of creating supervision to control it. Third, when it came to competing with the United States, France could equal Britain's political mistakes. Finally, Concorde is the product more of political will than of technical genius.

THE CONCORDE TALE

The history of Concorde has been told often, albeit for competing purposes. John Costello and Terry Hughes recount Concorde's development to argue that the United States conspired to keep the plane out of American airports and to kill the European aircraft industry.[5] Air Commodore John Davis emphasizes the military origins, collaborative calamities, and conflicting commercial obligations of the project.[6] Andrew Wilson argues that "it was politically irresponsible to start Concorde, wrong to continue it when its failure became apparent, and socially unforgivable to pour more than £1000 million into a jet-set plaything when the resources were so urgently needed for other tasks."[7] Richard Wiggs's purpose is no more disguised: His history of Concorde is designed to expose "grossly inadequate estimates of its cost . . . extravagant and insubstantial claims about its benefits and . . . refusal to face the facts about its anti-social effects."[8] Peter Hall considers Concorde a planning disaster.[9] Jean Forestier demonstrates that Concorde was a victim of transnational compromises,[10] and

François de Closets focuses on French hubris.[11] Annabelle May summarizes Concorde's history in an effort to prove that the source of the calamity in Britain was the excessive desire of the Foreign and Commonwealth Office (FCO) to use Concorde as a passport for entry into Europe.[12] Whatever the differences in interpretation of real costs and benefits of the project (astronomical expenditures vs. unlimited technical spin-off, environmental pollution vs. world technological leadership, successful collaboration vs. commercial failure, etc.), and whatever the differences in the purposes with which they write, Concorde's chroniclers generally agree on the basic chronology and ruinous cost escalation.

The state of the industries

When the French and British governments signed the treaty "regarding the development and production of a civil supersonic transport aircraft"[13] in November 1962, the British aircraft industry was three times larger than the French. The British had been investigating supersonic transport since 1956, and the Supersonic Transport Aircraft Committee (STAC) prepared a report "For British Eyes Only" in early 1959.[14] There is no evidence of any French thinking about supersonic transport before Aubrey Jones, then British minister of supply, proposed collaboration at the June 1959 Paris Air Show. An unnamed high-ranking British official, within the subsequent twelve months, delivered the STAC report (which remains classified and never has been released to the British Parliament) to the French. At the Paris Air Show in 1961, the French replied to Jones's proposal by displaying a model of a "Super Caravelle," a delta-winged supersonic transport not unlike the British model suggested by STAC.

The British industry was significantly more advanced than the French. Yet the treaty specified "equal sharing between the two countries, on the basis of equal responsibility for the project as a whole." This apparent British sacrifice has been the frequent target of criticism,[15] but both sides had plausible reasons for entering into the agreement. The French obviously saw an opportunity to advance their aircraft industry and achieve equality on the technical frontier with Europe's leading manufacturers. The successes of the Mirage and the Caravelle gave the French confidence in their ability to build marketable jet aircraft, but they also understood that their industry was too small to build supersonic transport on their own. The British, by contrast, were dispirited. They had beaten the Americans to a commercial jet, but the Comet flopped and the VC 10 had been criticized even by British Airways. With the additional failure of the Blue Streak, Jones had reckoned: "Were I as Minister to go to the Treasury the money would not be forthcoming. So . . . I went to France."[16] The United States then canceled Skybolt in 1962, reminding Britain that it did not fully control its own aviation and aerospace industry and could not rely on the Americans.[17] Hence, although the British had appeared to be ahead of the French, even within the aircraft industry itself there was cause to combine forces.

Political conditions

The condition most frequently cited as motivating the British to sacrifice their aviation lead by collaborating with France was the British desire to join Europe. Through early 1962 negotiations with France had not been promising, and officials responsible for the aircraft industry, strong Europeanists all, were keen to improve the situation. A June 1962 Macmillan–de Gaulle meeting was unexpectedly cordial, and the aviation project therefore climbed quickly on the agenda as a potential British contribution to European cooperation.

There can be no doubt that the European dimension was central to the conclusion of the treaty and the specification of its terms.[18] Nor can there be much doubt that de Gaulle exploited British anxieties to make the terms favorable for France. However, Concorde's claim to special citizenship reaches beyond the European passport and cannot explain the French commitment, since the British were the supplicants and the French were not necessarily interested in an expanded European community. Furthermore, cooperation extended well beyond the date of Britain's European entry, which was well after any illusions remained about profitability in the enterprise.

Britain and France both felt betrayed by the United States at Suez. The British already had approached the Americans unsuccessfully about cooperation in supersonic transport. Both British and French aircraft industries needed renewal. The Fifth Republic was shopping for high-profile prestige to bolster the regime, especially in science and technology. Above all, the French saw Concorde as a last best hope to preserve a European industry independent of the United States. Given the lead on supersonic transport established by the British, the French finally could defeat the Americans in a contest of great consequence.

The British Government, having just lost a series of by-elections, was anxious to reinvigorate the economy. Macmillan even had accelerated supersonic studies in 1959, hoping that development might absorb unemployment. Thus Britain's commitment to Europe cemented convictions formulated out of complex domestic and foreign concerns, and France's European advantage helped set the terms of project equality for what had begun with a British technical lead in an unequal partnership.

No exit

The 1962 treaty was never submitted to either country's parliament for ratification. No reliable cost estimates for a joint venture were generated before the signing, even though both parties entered into the contract in part because anticipated expenses would far exceed their separate budgets. Yet the agreement excluded an even more startling provision: No mechanism was mentioned permitting either Britain or France to withdraw. The British reasoned, first, that an escape clause could permit the French to pirate Britain's technical knowledge and then build their own plane and, second, that inscription of a divorce clause at the wedding could sour the marriage.

The French, for their part, continued to distrust British links to the United States and prudently denied rights in the marriage to any lovers. It was the British side, however, that insisted on the absence of a cancellation clause, and in particular it was Minister of Aviation Julian Amery (see Table 5.1, in the next chapter). Because the two governments were financing the project he rejected the idea of a commercial contract, and because of the heavy commitments of money and brains he did not think either side should be able to depart unilaterally. Most of all, he feared that the French might pull out. The British Treasury and the French Ministry of Finance both objected, but Amery prevailed.[19] The two countries were joined until death or, at least, as later interpretations insisted, until a prototype could fly.

The treaty was subjected to early modification. The terms stipulated the development of two different airplanes, one medium and the other long range, an objective mutually abandoned in early 1964 when no orders were placed for the more conservative French version (which was to be smaller and slower and to have shorter range) and options were taken by Pan American Airways on a long-range craft. Article 4 required "integrated organisations of the airframe and engine firms," a stipulation that hardly was satisfied by myriad joint committees. Nevertheless, the no-exit character of the treaty helped prevent cancellation when these and later modifications were the subject of harsh negotiations.

On at least four specific occasions Britain wanted to abandon the project, and there were more frequent high-level reservations. The French were similarly inclined at least three times, but not at the same times as the British. The British concerns were expressed publicly; the French were more secretive. This difference, more than any other, contributed to the impression that the British were nervous or stingy (or both) while the French had more confidence and commitment.

The British made open exit plans in 1964, spring 1967, 1970, and 1974. Labour's first objective after its election in October 1964 was to cancel expensive prestige projects planned or begun by the Conservatives. Concorde, TSR-2 (the Tactical Strike Reconnaissance plane under construction by the British manufacturers of Concorde), and two other military aircraft were at the top of Labour's list. Prime Minister Harold Wilson believed that he had inherited a full economic crisis from the Tories, and he expected a balance-of-payments deficit of $1.96 billion for that year. There were innuendos from Washington of help on the balance of payments if Concorde were abandoned (for the U.S. industry did not welcome costly competition), and Wilson was not an eager European. Moreover, two months after the treaty had been signed, de Gaulle again had closed the door to British entry into Europe. Yet despite all these incentives against Concorde, the military planes were canceled and Concorde survived, chiefly because the French reminded the new British Government that both parties were bound by a treaty enforceable in the Hague. The objective, to avoid pending expenditures, could be offset by penalties reaching as high as $560 million – more than Britain's predicted share in 1964 for completing the whole project. French industry had not yet acquired the British technology promised by collaboration and was not willing, therefore, to give up.

Invocation of the treaty, de Gaulle's reference to Concorde as a symbol of Anglo-French cooperation in his January 1963 speech barring Britain from the EEC, and consequent damages for treaty violation were not the only dissuading factors. The British manufacturers threatened to close a major factory, thereby rallying trade unions against cancellation. The Labour Government subsequently proposed a compromise that would limit commitments to two prototypes, but the French again refused. When the Cabinet finally accepted defeat on cancellation, it was more to avoid humiliation before the International Court than even the financial damages or the blow to friendship with France. And union pressure, at the heart of Labour's political strength, was important.[20]

There has been unconfirmed speculation that the French Ministry of Finance also wanted to cancel in early 1965 and that even at Sud Aviation, the French airframe manufacturer, there was considerable uncertainty about the wisdom of pressing ahead. Henri Ziegler, later the plane's leading champion, questioned the project in a private 1966 report. But the French avoided communicating publicly any possibility of cancellation lest they compromise their bargaining position with the plaintiff British, and their trade union leaders joined British union officials in support of the project.

Devaluation of the pound sterling in 1967 triggered another Cabinet-level review, but again defense cuts preserved Concorde alone among major aircraft projects. The future of the British industry had come to depend on Concorde. The Cabinet was conscious that Concorde was a high-profile undertaking that not only could affect an international image but also contributed to domestic pride. Most important, perhaps, the key minister in 1967, Anthony Wedgwood Benn, represented a Bristol constituency where twenty-one thousand workers were building the prototype.

The Conservative electoral victory in June 1970 precipitated another review. This time a fear of increased unemployment was the leading obstacle to cancellation, with 25 percent of Britain's aircraft industry working on Concorde. Prime Minister Edward Heath also was keen for Britain finally to join the European communities. Above all, the Tories wanted to press ahead with a series of high-profile, labor-intensive public works. The agenda included new motorways, the chunnel, Maplin, and Concorde.

While Heath's government reconsidered Concorde in Britain, Count Charles de Chambrun, a prominent Gaullist deputy in the National Assembly, offered privately to the French government a report firmly recommending abandonment of the project. In the climate of French élite consensus, however, no final reconsideration was possible, especially as the American SST project was still under way.[21]

The final serious cancellation efforts came in 1974. Again Anthony Wedgwood Benn was the key figure, and money was the key issue. The options taken by foreign airlines had been dropped, so that there was little hope of selling Concorde outside Britain and France. The 1971 bankruptcy of Rolls Royce and various strikes in Britain beginning in 1972 had slowed production, which had been retarded already by the events of May 1968 in France and the subsequent devaluation of the franc. The American SST program had been killed in 1971, and officials no longer had a challenge to meet, but they did fear that the United States would discourage airlines from flying Concorde. Of the sixteen aircraft planned in the production line, orders stood for only nine, all destined – through government instruction – for the national airlines of the manufacturing countries. It was believed widely that Prime Minister Heath's own Central Policy Review Staff wanted to cancel at the end of 1973, and the Department of Trade and Industry no longer believed that sales would ever exceed thirty aircraft. The Tories began to negotiate important design modifications with the French in February 1974, hoping to reduce the noise they thought could bar the Concorde from essential ports of call, and then delayed further discussions pending the British general elections.

The Department of Industry prepared a devastating report for the new minister, who with the Labour victory was Benn. Benn told Bristol workers, "If Concorde fails it would be a national disaster and a tragedy for Bristol."[22] Subsequently, he offered to the House of Commons a candid review of Concorde's finances that strongly implied cancellation. British Airways predicted that it would lose money operating the plane, and Pan American Airways indicated that it would not want the plane even if it were given away. Ten percent of the entire manufacturing labor force in southwest England was working on Concorde, and once again the industry campaigned against cancellation. British Aircraft Corporation (BAC) printed five hundred thousand copies of "The Common Sense of Concorde" for national distribution, and in June the prototype was rushed out for "proving flights" to generate popular support.

The French also sought cancellation in 1974, but not precisely when it seemed feasible to the British. The French also wanted to delay for elections. Nevertheless, a compelling case for cancellation had emerged. The Airbus was behind schedule and was receiving few orders. The Mercure was a commercial failure with only one buyer, the French Air Inter, who acquired the only ten ever produced; it cost more, and delivered less, than the 727 or the DC-9. General René Bloch of Dassault-Breguet, not one of Concorde's manufacturers, had reported to the government privately in December 1973 that Concorde could succeed only if it were virtually rebuilt at spectacular public expense; he predicted a maximum sale of thirty-three planes. The general economy was sputtering in the first international oil crisis.

President Pompidou's health was failing. His government did not want to risk public embarrassment through the cancellation of such a prestige project just before elections. The aircraft industry union leaders had joined the British campaign to save the plane, and Aérospatiale, the manufacturer, insisted that it would sell 130 planes. The French Communist Party (PCF) had threatened to approach the Soviet Union to pursue the plane's development, and Georges Marchais, the PCF leader, had called cancellation "inadmissible" because the French aircraft industry had no certain alternative for manufacture. The political consequences of immediate cancellation overrode economic logic.

Jean-Jacques Servan-Schreiber, a strident foe of Concorde's development, left the government after the spring elections. Marcel Cavaillé, an enthusiastic supporter of Concorde, became the new secretary of state for transport and civil aviation. Jacques Chirac had campaigned for France's presidency with a pledge to increase Concorde's production, but Valéry Giscard d'Estaing had promised only to finish the series under way. The new president prevailed, securing agreement with the newly elected Wilson at meetings in July. Whereas earlier ministerial meetings might have led to immediate termination, such meetings had been postponed because of President Pompidou's death.

Wilson had already canceled Maplin when he met with Giscard, and indeed it was the termination of one major project that made continuation of the other viable. Such had been the case a decade earlier when this same prime minister had canceled TSR-2 only to save Concorde. Giscard, meanwhile, could observe that, as in Britain, 25 percent of the French aircraft industry was working on Concorde and that it would be wiser to wind down the project than to cancel it outright. The plane was becoming known in the British Departments of Trade and Industry as an albatross, but it might as easily have been called a phoenix.

Industrial existentialism

By the late 1960s the cost, if not the plane, was soaring. Various reasons are offered, but there is some essential agreement. The escalation jumped at certain points, and these jumps coincided three times with the major redesign of the aircraft, in 1963, 1965, and 1967. The new designs involved responses to the plane's commercial requirements, which had been ignored almost systematically by the engineers. They had been preoccupied with flying a large frame supersonically, not with the comfort of passengers (the narrow fuselage would leave minimal walking and head room) or fuel costs that would determine viable operations for the most promising routes.

Other explanations for cost escalation include inflation,[23] devaluations,[24] the inability to forecast requirements of a whole new technology,[25] and the absence of Finance and Treasury controls. The project had been given military priority because of the potential application of the technology, and it formally came under military supervision. Such arrangements guaranteed the secrecy a strictly commercial project could not justify, and there was consequently a notorious inclination to spend carelessly. Suggestions emerged that both French and British manufacturers ran up the bills, knowing that the partner would have to pick up half.[26] More simply, however, France and Britain had embarked upon an unprecedented task, technically, politically, and commercially; they had little basis for anticipating costs and estimates rarely were based on careful calculations. Furthermore, both governments gave their respective industries effective *carte blanche* on Concorde. As other aviation projects foundered or were canceled, energies were channeled increasingly into this lone enterprise. All the hopes, dreams, and purses for research and development of the aircraft industry in Britain and France came to depend upon Concorde.

As Concorde became vital to the industries, they saw themselves as vital to their countries. The plane, they reasoned, would have to be accepted by the national airlines, and once entered into commercial service it would be irresistible to airline competitors. Consequently, cost and commercial viability were far less important to the engineers than the technical achievement. A senior engineer for Air France thus has called the cost escalation and extended development "industrial existentialism."[27]

There allegedly were important differences in Britain and France in attitude toward cost. Milton S. Hochmuth has pointed out that Concorde was an adventure for the future in France, and advances in technology did not invite cost control. By contrast, the British sacrificed their superior technological position because they needed the work Concorde provided; because it was an economic move, it could not be permitted to run as extravagant a course as it was taking in France.[28] However, as in all other aspects of this case, the two countries had occasion to exchange positions on expenditures.

In early 1960 British manufacturers themselves had begun designing two different supersonic transports. The smaller, medium-range plane (100 passengers, 1,500 miles at Mach 1.2) would cost $168–$196 million, and the larger, long-range model (150 passengers, 3,500 miles at Mach 1.8) would cost $252 million. Two years later, when the Anglo-French Treaty for two planes was signed, internal estimates suggested some $475 million, including construction of two prototypes and two pre-production aircraft; the British share would be half, much less than the anticipated cost of the project for Britain working alone.

The contracts to the manufacturers were cost-plus, with the governments paying all the bills. There were no incentives to control expenses. To work on Concorde was to enjoy unlimited funds, substantial prestige, and the excitement and challenge of new technology.[29] When the challenge was formidable the budget simply grew, so that by 1966 it consumed 70 percent of France's entire civil aircraft development resources.

Concorde was a government undertaking. Unlike other commercial aircraft in development, it had no airline sponsor, and indeed the airlines were not consulted when the first crucial planning was done. Air France, from the outset, preferred development of the Caravelle, and the British carriers were little interested in any British plane (save, perhaps, the BAC 111).

The 1963 design changes followed first responses from the airlines. The British manufacturers had attracted options from Pan American Airways and strong interest from many other airlines; the French manufacturers had attracted no buyers. The British envisioned routes across the Atlantic with a larger plane; the French envisioned overland routes such as Paris–Algiers. Without reference to noise, which neither British nor French manufacturers considered important, the attractiveness of the plane clearly would depend partly upon airline calculations of its usefulness for potential routes. The French reluctantly gave in to the British preferences.

The first redesign, to produce a single plane, yielded a new estimate of $770 million, up from $475 million for two different planes. In late 1965, with a second redesign to increase fuel capacity and passenger load, the estimate reached $1.4 billion. Projected weight of the plane also rose from 149 to 160 tons. The 1967 design changes then led to a 1968 estimate of $1.68 billion, and in 1969 the official estimate reached $1.75 billion for a plane of 170 tons. Details of these costs were never made public (owing to the official secrecy of the project), but rolling out the prototype a full year later had not helped, and each increase in weight implied a sacrifice in passenger space. The plane's capacity was shrinking from an initial estimate of 140 seats to a configuration of 100 or fewer.

In the March 1974 review the British predicted losing $540 million if they were to produce the sixteen planned aircraft, for the flight test and production program was already costing Britain $3.6 million every week. Through December 31, 1976, Concorde had actually cost $2.43 billion, and an additional $317 million was estimated as necessary to bring the program to completion over the subsequent twenty-four months. By the end of 1978, excluding research, the British and French governments had *each* spent $2.25 billion (ten times the 1960 estimates), and then the British had spent $350 million to buy the plane from the manufacturer for British Airways. Of course, the $2.25 billion already represented money paid by the British government to the manufacturer to build the plane. The government counted the $350 million for the purchase as in-

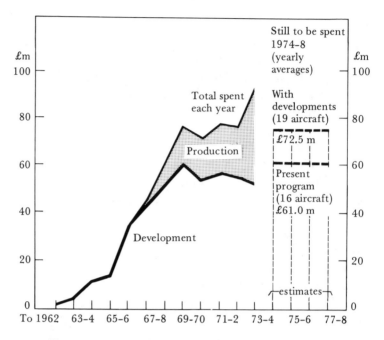

Figure 4.1. Concorde: the 1974 review of costs. Redrawn from The Economist *250 (1974), p. 71.*

come from the Concorde program (on costs see Figs. 4.1 and 4.2).

The end of production did not mean the end of the cost. Pledged to the maintenance of the planes in operation, British Airways organized a complete parts stock at each Concorde station; in 1976 the Washington, D.C., stock, for example, was worth $2.2 million, and it was duplicated in Bahrain and later in Dallas, New York, and, for Air France, Rio, Dakar, and Caracas. Furthermore, as we shall see, both governments were pledged to subsidize operating losses for their national airlines flying Concorde, and the Concorde losses had a way of escalating and accumulating. The main difference from the prior experience of such escalation, however, was that the airlines fully predicted such costs and said that they did not want to buy or fly Concorde.

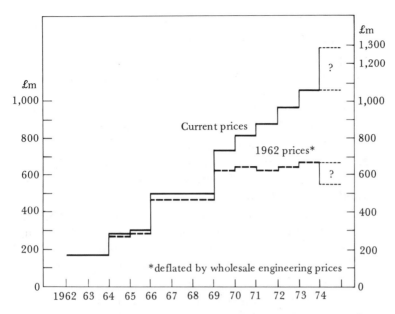

Figure 4.2. Government estimates through 1974 of the combined cost to Britain and France of developing Concorde. Redrawn from The Economist *250 (1974), p. 71.*

The plum becomes a prune

The industrial commitment to Concorde, driven by government agreements and government guarantees, had a profound multiplier effect, especially in Britain. The aircraft industries in Britain and France expended national treasuries only to leave themselves further behind the Americans than when they began. The most promising marketable enterprise, the Airbus, was several years late because of Concorde,[30] and other promising projects, such as an advanced Caravelle, were sacrificed. In Britain Concorde's engine manufacturer was presented through government negotiation with the largest single export sale in British history, hailed in the *Financial Times* as "the most succulent trade plum of the century." But the deal was not for Concorde's already technologically backward Olympus engines, and the burden of Concorde combined with this additional commitment to humble Britain's proudest and most prestigious industrial name. Rolls Royce, manufacturer of Concorde's engines, merged with Bristol-Siddeley in 1966. The latter was a debt-ridden company the Labour Government was determined to save. The Government therefore was delighted to announce on March 30, 1968, that Rolls Royce (now the parent company) had outbid General Electric to build the RB 211 engine for the Lockheed TriStar L1011. The initial order for 540 engines was valued at $2.5 billion.

The Lockheed Corporation entered this agreement while carrying a cost overrun of $758 million on the C-5A military transport. No settlement had yet been reached with the Pentagon. Thus both aircraft and the engine manufacturers were private corporations desperately trying to climb out of debt because of prior or ongoing monumental project failures. The roots of the tree bearing the succulent plum were financially rotten, and the recipient already suffered from indigestion.

By February 1971 both Lockheed and Rolls Royce had collapsed. Originally estimated to cost $156 million per engine, the RB 211 had reached $408 million in less than three years. The official inquiry later concluded: "The size of the engineering task was seriously underestimated. From this basic fact flowed the appalling consequences . . . Once the contract was signed, no system of financial control could have significantly influenced the course of events." As with Concorde, "The personalities on the financial side were outgunned by those on the engineering side."[31]

When the first sense of crisis descended upon Rolls Royce in November 1970, the corporation proposed abandoning the RB 211. Lockheed, perhaps learning from the French, demanded respect for the contract. President Richard Nixon said that he would not help the ailing U.S. manufacturer. The British Government then contributed $150 million to a Rolls rescue, which lasted only three months. Nixon and

Prime Minister Edward Heath conferred in February and agreed to a bail-out, which for Rolls Royce meant a government take-over of the company's essential assets and an official bankruptcy. The very symbol of British wealth and stability, often compared to the rock of Gibraltar, cracked beyond recognition into a public enterprise.

The prime minister, explaining the take-over, said: "We are ensuring the safety and efficiency of our armed services as well as those of 81 air forces and more than 200 airlines overseas, all operating with Rolls Royce engines."[32] Indeed, the combination of Concorde – a deal with the French – and the RB 211 – a deal with Americans – had broken Europe's leading and the world's most respected manufacturer of aircraft engines. And ironically, as the Concorde engine was the noisiest for a new plane, the RB 211 was the quietest. Each had required substantial technological innovation, and the single corporation developing aircraft engines simultaneously for speed, quiet, and economy could meet the technical but not the fiscal challenge. The private corporation, conscious of this dilemma, had wanted to stop, but state interest, which accorded fiscal consideration secondary importance, pressed ahead. The industrial existentialism that had taken over the Concorde tale was carried by the state throughout the prestigious aviation sector.

The albatross

By 1975 Britain's Department of Trade was responsible for selling the Concorde that the Department of Industry and the Ministry of Defence were responsible for building. The price had been settled by British and French transport ministers (who neither built the plane nor would have to sell it) in December 1971 when production schedules had been committed to 10 planes immediately, with 6 to follow and subsequent production to fill anticipated orders from 74 options. No attempt would be made to recover any research and development investment; the manufacturing cost was to be recovered, without profit, by setting the unit cost against projected construction of 150 aircraft. Even then, the price was related more to the market price for the Boeing 747 (under $30 million) than to precise estimates of assembly line costs for Concorde.

The price of $31.2 million assumed that at least 50 Concordes would be in service to spread the costs of maintenance and spare parts. Airlines were promised a break-even point on operations with a load factor of 35.5 percent, contrasted to 44 percent for the Boeing 747.[33] Assumptions included constant navigation and landing fees, pilot wages consistent with those for other commercial aircraft, and fuel at 13.9 cents per U.S. gallon.

The Concorde's range, limited to 3,650 statute miles fully loaded as the product of technical design compromises, limited potential routes and therefore potential users. The number of seats, with adjustments for climate, season, and distance, could not exceed 112 and could fall in some circumstances below 100. Indeed, during the 1976 heat wave in Britain, take-offs were delayed up to five hours and the maximum payload to Washington, D.C., fell to 71 passengers. During an average crossing of the Atlantic, the plane would burn nearly 172,000 pounds of fuel, or 5,380 imperial gallons per hour. At 1974 prices, Concorde's fuel cost over $3,500 per hour and represented more than half the plane's weight. British Airways estimated Concorde's cost per seat-mile, projected to 1977 from 1974, to be more than three times the cost for a Boeing 747 (see Fig. 4.3).

Concorde, then, could not fly very far and promised to be expensive to operate. The noise it generated, moreover, far exceeded that of all subsonic aircraft being licensed in the 1970s (see Fig. 4.4). The sonic boom persuaded the airlines and airport authorities that the plane could not utilize its supersonic capability over populated areas. Gordon Davidson, Concorde director for British Airways, said in 1976, "Concorde routes have to be over water or desert because of the bang . . . you have to find

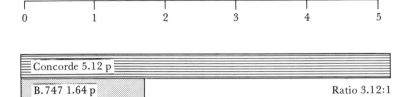

Figure 4.3. Concorde versus Boeing 747: comparisons of costs per seat-mile (all classes of travel), projected to 1977 from 1974. Redrawn from British Airways, "Concorde Appraisal" (Mimeographed, 1974).

two points where the market is highly business-dominated that are separated mostly by water or desert."[34]

The Department of Trade was responsible in Britain for marketing Concorde. It proved an impossible task. British Airways, already having criticized Britain's most promising commercial plane, the VC 10, wanted no part of Concorde. Conditions had changed since Sir Giles Guthrie, then chairman of BOAC, had called for immediate mass production in 1967. By the time decisions had to be made for production (in 1967 only completion of the technological tests was at issue), it was apparent that optimistic predictions for operating costs were inaccurate. British Airways was asked by the Department of Trade to report fully on its view of the plane's future, and David L. Nicolson's reply on behalf of the British Airways board to the secretary of state for trade was clear and blunt: "The conditions and assumptions necessary for profitable Concorde services are not those on which a commercial management could prudently plan its future operations."[35] If British Airways were to be forced to fly Concorde, Nicolson wrote, the British government had better be ready to pick up the bill.

Air France had refused to participate in the plane's development lest it be obliged through such cooperation to buy the plane. It was so obliged despite its diffidence. Transport Minister Marc Jacquet informed the national airline's director that when the plane was ready Air France

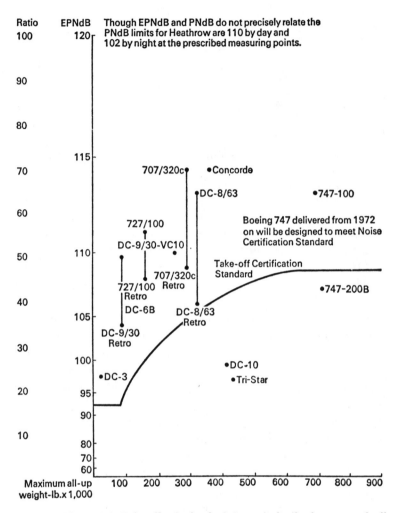

Figure 4.4. Take-off noise levels, 3.5 nautical miles from start of roll on extended runway center line (EPNdB = Effective Perceived Noise Decibels; PNdB = Perceived Noise Decibels; the two measures reflect variations in the time when the aircraft is in the vicinity). Reprinted by permission of the author from Andrew Wilson, The Concorde Fiasco *(Harmondsworth: Penguin Books, 1973), p. 116.*

was to buy it in appreciation of its "national importance."[36] This instruction had become necessary because Air France had been persuaded by an engineer's report, dated October 11, 1960, that the costs of development were incalculable, the plane's weight would raise doubt about operating costs, and the noise probably would deny flights over populated areas. The government would have to force the flag carrier to operate Concorde.

If the flag carriers did not want Concorde, even at special subsidized prices that wrote off research and development, why would other airlines buy it? With the American SST cancellation in April 1971, most airlines concluded that they did not want Concorde, and by late 1972, *before the first oil shock,* most options were dropped. Lufthansa, for example, estimated in 1972 that the plane could not make New York from Frankfurt with more than sixty-one passengers and their baggage; modifications to increase the payload would cost at least another $400 million and would be impossible on the first sixteen planes already committed to production. Japan Airlines, interested in a route linking Tokyo to Anchorage, discovered that the plane's range was inadequate. British and French marketing hopes came to depend entirely on the belief that foreign, and especially U.S., airlines would be forced to compete with British Airways and Air France and therefore would eventually have to buy the plane. The manufacturing countries reasoned that Concorde would skim off first-class traffic on major routes. Despite the warnings from their own airlines, British and French manufacturers and governments accordingly proceeded on the commitment to a minimum of sixteen aircraft.

CONCORDE IN SERVICE

Routes

Concorde's potential routes were defined by its range. The original British vision, to sell a supersonic aircraft to U.S.

carriers for transcontinental travel, had been destroyed by
the reality of Concorde's noise. In August 1973 senior executives of BAC urged their French colleagues to join in
solving the noise problem at whatever cost. Despite the
popular image that the British were financially prudent
and the French extravagant in Concorde's development, it
was the French who refused a further investment that would
respond to a perceived requirement of commercial viability. The French reasoned that noise was a political, not a
technical, problem, and it should be negotiated politically.
Moreover, the French said, it would be too expensive to
find a technical solution.[37] But noise indeed restricted operations, and therefore sales, as suggested by British Airways' Gordon Davidson.[38]

The most obvious and important routes would link Europe and the United States, the world's leading air passenger markets. Range and noise would confine supersonic
operations to the East Coast, and the Europeans were most
eager to fly from capital to capital (London and Paris to
Washington) and between the largest markets (New York
and the European capitals). U.S. opposition, however, was
intense, and although access to Washington was granted
by the Federal Aviation Administration (FAA), no nonfed-
eral airport in the United States would allow regular flights.

Other routes were less attractive but no less complicated.
Concorde promised to reduce travel time significantly, but
over very long distances it would have to stop and refuel.
Boeing's 747SP, with a nonstop capability exceeding ten
thousand miles, could reach Sydney from London faster
than Concorde and at a fraction of the cost. From London
or Paris, Johannesburg required at least one stop for Concorde, as did Tokyo, Rio de Janeiro, and Mexico City.
Tehran lost its promise as the shah's regime weakened and
fell, and Iran Air ceased to be a potential buyer. The manufacturers had calculated potential sales on the assumption that the plane could go anywhere; airlines, calculating
ticket prices and markets against the specific advantages of
the plane, knew better.

The route to Australia called for stops in Bahrain, a small Arab state on the Persian Gulf, and Singapore, with flights over densely populated areas in Lebanon, India, Sumatra, and Java. The Indians refused overflight permission, and access to Singapore was denied (a subsequent reversal through a complex agreement with Singapore Airlines did not ultimately solve the problem). Concorde could get to Bahrain, but no further. No black African country would permit Concorde to stop for the purpose of serving South African businessmen. Even with generous offers to improve the airport in Lagos, the British could not persuade any country to open the route. Johannesburg could not be reached.

Tokyo required a stop in the Soviet Union. The Tupolev, a poor copy of Concorde (indeed, often called "Concordski"), failed technically, first by crashing at the Paris Air Show and killing six civilians in Goussainville. Subsequent trials in the Soviet Union did not yield satisfactory results. The Russians were not interested in helping the Europeans establish a commercial operation that would mock Soviet technology. Moreover, the route required supersonic overflight of densely populated areas in the Soviet Union. Tokyo could not be reached.

British Airways, when Concorde entered commercial service in 1976, had five of the aircraft and access only to Bahrain. The French situation was not much better. Access to Rio de Janeiro was established by flying through Dakar from Paris, and Caracas was reached through the Azores. None of these destinations could justify more than two or three round-trip flights per week. Hence Concorde could not prove itself to potential competitors in commercial operation, and British Airways and Air France could not operate their nine aircraft enough to earn any money.

Access to the United States

Access for Concorde to New York became the single most important objective for the foreign policies of Britain and

France in their relations with the United States. Pressure was brought by the British prime minister and the French president directly on the president of the United States. European journalists and politicians accused the United States of a conspiracy to destroy the European aircraft industry, first by the refusal of U.S. carriers to buy Concorde and then by denying access to the world's most important passenger markets.

Leaders of the fight against the American SST, especially organizations such as Friends of the Earth, mobilized against Concorde. The European plane would not pollute less, use less fuel, or make less noise than the planned Boeing version. Therefore, according to this lobby, it made no more sense to let Concorde fly to U.S. cities than it did to finance development of a U.S. plane. Airport neighbors in New York were enraged over the prospects of Concorde operations, and U.S. carriers, though sympathetic to the principle that any commercial aircraft ought to be able to operate anywhere, were decidedly unenthusiastic about a plane that conceivably could hurt their first-class passenger business yet make no profit for any operator. British environmental lobbyists, finally, rallied to the cause of their U.S. counterparts, contributing to an American image of the plane as more French than British.

The British and the French won in U.S. courts, and Kennedy International Airport began allowing regular Concorde operations in 1977. The French had been highly confrontational in the impasse with authorities in New York, insisting that the White House could dictate access to all U.S. ports. Considerable ill will was generated between New Yorkers and Parisians, and between government leaders in Washington and Paris, because of a fundamental French failure to appreciate the complexities of American federalism. Indeed, French officials believed that "any bunch of hippies plus lawyers could be stronger than the signature of Uncle Sam himself on any air transport agreement,"[39] and they interpreted this version of democratic control as a weakness in international affairs. The British, by contrast, far more accustomed to adjustment for apparently popular protest, believed that they could use U.S. legal and judicial procedures rather than political negotiation. They lowered their profile, contributing still further to the impression that Concorde was a French plane. Nowhere in the history of Concorde was the contrast between the British and the French greater than in their direct dealings with the Americans. Both were committed to competing with the United States, but the French wanted the glory of victory, whereas the British would settle for the satisfaction of penetrating the U.S. market. Nevertheless, their cause was common and their tactics complementary. The British, as in many previous instances, were more correct in their calculations and more successful in the outcome, but the greatest impression continued to be of contrast and French superiority.

Much of the expected protest in New York did not materialize once Concorde began regular flights. Although the noise in the nearby neighborhoods still exceeded that of other aircraft, and although mysterious sonic booms all along the East Coast ultimately were attributed to Concorde's approach, official monitor readings could not support damage claims. Air France and British Airways pilots were instructed to take off from Kennedy International Airport with steep turns that would avoid the FAA noise monitors, and Concorde proved a supple and maneuverable aircraft.[40] Nevertheless, the U.S. court victory was pyrrhic, for the New York route, perhaps operationally profitable at the margins, only delayed the inevitable.

CONCORDE'S FINAL DAYS

By 1978 production of Concordes had stopped, the manufacture of spare parts had been reduced sharply, and the French and British had entered into discussions that eventually will establish a mutual date for the termination of commercial Concorde operations during the 1980s. Singapore Airlines briefly shared with British Airways Concorde routes in the Far East, and Braniff briefly operated Concorde subsonically between Dulles and Dallas, hoping to pick up Texas oilmen for a swift crossing of the Atlantic. Both experiments failed. Federal Express, the American cargo carrier, has contemplated leasing the two idle Concordes for transatlantic overnight deliveries. No other airline has wanted the plane; Pan American Airways even rejected an essentially free lease. An Air France official remarked, when his airline paid a nominal franc for each of three more planes (the final delivery, bringing the Air France fleet to seven), "They certainly are not worth much more than that. One franc apiece would be too much."[41]

By the end of 1978, $4.28 billion had been spent to build two prototypes and fourteen commercial planes. Each Concorde cost $267 million, and from the initial $31.2 million price tag to the $80 million final purchase price, the plane was essentially given away. Indeed, most of the money to buy the planes was given by the British and French governments to their national airlines, so that transfers of money remained on government books with no gain for government treasuries.

In the first operating year British Airways lost $11 million on Concorde; Air France lost $44 million because it flew more often. Concorde's losses climbed in proportion to operating hours, yet if any of the purchase price were to be recaptured the plane would need more flying time. British Airways actually calculated a need for each Concorde in its fleet to fly a minimum of 2,500 hours per year. With a transatlantic crossing of 3 hours and 45 minutes, the plane would have had to fly round trip 333 days per year, a schedule barely allowing for maintenance. This estimate, moreover, did not recognize the substantial premium won by Concorde pilots, nor the sharp escalation of fuel prices later in the decade (see Fig. 4.5). It is difficult to imagine more than two such daily round-trip operations

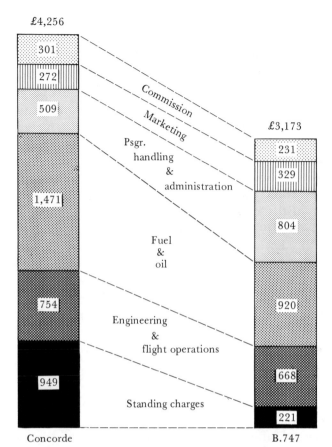

£4,256

301
272
509

1,471

754

949

Commission
Marketing

Psgr.
handling
&
administration

Fuel
&
oil

Engineering
&
flight operations

Standing charges

£3,173

231
329

804

920

668
221

Concorde

B.747

Comparison	Concorde	B.747
Average utilization (hours per year)	2,825	4,850
Configuration	100 one class	27 first class/ 379 coach
Fare level applied	F to F + 20%	F/Y normal
Seat factor assumed (% of seats expected to be filled on the average)	55	56

Figure 4.5. Concorde versus Boeing 747: total costs per flying hour, 1977–8 ("F to F + 20%" indicates indecision: Fares would be either all first class or – the final choice – first class with 20% supplement; "F/Y normal" indicates first class and coach without supplement). Redrawn from British Airways, "Concorde Appraisal" (Mimeographed, 1974).

of this exclusive first-class service, and then only to New York (a limit that both Air France and British Airways calculated from market studies). There could be no operational logic in a fleet of Concordes, and there was no financial logic in maintaining only two or three planes.

Increased production of the plane would have meant increased losses. According to 1974 estimates reported by Anthony Wedgwood Benn to the House of Commons, British losses would have escalated to $180 million for the construction of thirty-five Concordes.

Increased operations of Concorde also meant greater losses. British Airways reported in 1977 a 50 percent loss in subsonic first-class passengers on Concorde routes. Instead of new passengers, the airline was merely gaining the difference in the price increment between first-class and luxury class. Air France had lost over $120 million operating Concorde through 1979, with fuel costs in control of the economics of the plane. By the end of 1979 seven Concordes represented 25 percent of the total fleet-operating costs for Air France.

Passenger growth did not help Concorde. British Airways could carry 100 passengers to Bahrain, but in the desert heat it could take off with only 70. Even then, average loads fell below 50 percent by 1978. Air France carried only between 35 percent and 40 percent to Caracas, and less than 40 percent to Washington despite continuing on to Mexico City beginning in late 1978. Even the Paris–New York route fell below 70 percent. British Airways, sometimes averaging 90 percent to New York, had the only profitable route and could not fly it often enough to make a single Concorde genuinely worthwhile.

By 1981 British Airways had given up the financially unsound sorties to Bahrain, thereby abandoning the dream of Concorde down under. The London–Washington route, later extended to Miami in yet another effort to find transatlantic passengers, had been reduced to three round trips per week. With the plane only half full, continuation of this route was doubtful. Two daily round trips to New York

– the only promising operation in the system – were carrying an average of 88 passengers (when 108 seats were available on the average, depending on climate). By now British Airways owned seven planes.

Air France reluctantly decided in early 1981 to give up direct flights to Washington. Braniff had abandoned the route to Dallas, and there were no other sources for passengers to fill the transatlantic flight. Eleven round trips per week were routed through New York City, with two continuing subsonically to Dulles and two others to Mexico City. The extensions soon stopped, and the trips to Rio and Caracas ended in April 1982. Privately, Air France President Pierre Giraudet wished that he did not have to fly the plane. Publicly, he said that it was up to the government and expressed pride in his country's technological achievement.

Both Air France and British Airways persuaded their governments that Concorde operations made no commercial sense and that the cost of prestige would have to be borne by those insisting they fly the plane. Starting in 1981 the French government increased its subsidy for Concorde deficits from 70 percent to 90 percent. The government bore the costs of promoting this symbol of French technological prowess, so the airline happily let advertising for Concorde dominate Air France's public image in the United States, despite the hostility engendered by the New York access fight. British Airways, meanwhile, had two more planes imposed on it, and in turn obligated the government to compensate all operating losses. The government paid for these planes and pledged the maintenance costs, expected to exceed $160 million over four years. Even under these terms British Caledonian had refused to accept a single Concorde. Sir Frederick Corfield, the responsible minister of aviation supply in 1970–1, reflected near the end of the decade, "With hindsight it is clear that the Concorde should not have been continued. The markets simply weren't there."[42]

British and French planners in 1964 projected 1,370

Concordes linking all the world's major cities. Within a decade of commercial introduction, however, there may be no Concordes flying commercially. Of the 16 finally built, Air France and British Airways each own 7 but fly no more than 4 and usually fewer. The other 2 of the 16 could become cargo transports, hardly the luxury craft that would enable one-day business trips between London and New York, San Francisco and Mexico City, Hong Kong and Singapore.[43]

Concorde's failure commonly is attributed to environmental protest, or the oil crisis, or the incompatibilities of the British and the French. Yet the impediment of noise did not even prevent Concorde from operating in three of the world's most environmentally sensitive cities, New York, Washington, and London. The collapse in sales and options preceded the oil shocks. And although styles and strategies often seemed to differ, the British and the French collaborated successfully enough to launch a supersonic transport with remarkable technical accuracy while the world's preeminent aircraft manufacturer, with the support of the government of the United States, still had merely a cardboard mock-up. Explanations for failure, then, must be found elsewhere.

PLANNING FOR THE SUPERSONIC AGE

The prospects of supersonic transport contributed to the perception that new aviation infrastructure, with new design, would be required for the last quarter of the twentieth century. Nevertheless, French and British planners looked more to political instruction than to projected technological change in formulating proposals for new airports. Beyond initial terminal design for Charles de Gaulle Airport and modest speculation about the impact of noise, there was no specific planning for the impact of supersonic transport in either Britain or France.

The aircraft itself did not involve specific planning either.

Once aeronautical engineers promised that they could produce a supersonic transport if they were given enough money and enough time, political commitment to the execution of the construction task dominated the development process. No one but the manufacturers had to cooperate, for the task was much narrower than the construction of an airport, even if the technological challenge was greater. The international treaty, only ten short paragraphs (one and one-half pages of type), enunciated a simple mandate for aircraft development by specific manufacturers: "The technical proposals . . . form the basis for the joint undertaking" (Article 3). A binational standing committee was formed to oversee the project. Members uniformly were project advocates prepared in both countries to hide escalating costs until revelation before their governments became unavoidable. Their disagreements over leadership of the project's components were sorted out by the unquestioned superiority of Rolls Royce (which took over Bristol-Siddeley after the treaty designating the latter as the engine manufacturer had been signed) and the forcefulness of Henri Ziegler and others working for Aérospatiale (which absorbed Sud Aviation, the treaty's French airframe designee). Periodic negotiations between ministers and even prime ministers were necessitated by technical recommendations for design changes (which escalated costs) or by appeals from one country or the other for cancellation of the entire project. Normally, however, engineers from the paired companies (Société Nationale d'Etudes et Construction de Moteurs Aviation [SNECMA] and Bristol-Siddeley for the engines, BAC and Sud Aviation for the airframe) shared their expertise while supervising independent manufacture on each side of the Channel. Ingenious technical solutions to problems were introduced, such as a specially designed plane to ferry large parts between Britain and France, but all such activity was concentrated on the manufacture of a specific product.

A planning process might have been appropriate for the

future of the plane, but both countries relied more on chance and faith. They believed that U.S. production of an SST guaranteed a market, so they did not sell Concorde systematically. Options taken by many airlines seemed to support this faith, but there were no contingency plans for a U.S. cancellation. As manufacturers, the two countries left to potential buyers the task of designing a systematic route structure. British and French planners preferred merely to suggest routes that unrealistically seemed to connect almost every major city in the world. Inasmuch as they were not to be the operators of the plane, and they thought it appropriate to dismiss the plane's operational liabilities (such as noise and fuel consumption) until the final redesign discussions, they did not plan a strategy for gaining access to the cities designated. All these problems were left to the airlines, which, aside from the British and French flag carriers, concluded simply that the required effort could never be justified. Hence implementation of a construction program was the sole objective; plans for the product were not formulated systematically in either country.

Only after cancellation of the American SST did product marketing become important to the French and British. Whereas one might have expected the French to develop systematic plans, it was the British who assessed the product carefully and concluded that more money would have to be invested to improve the product itself; the French, far more cavalier in the matter, assumed that buyers would have to accept the plane whatever its flaws: So much for one of the oldest stereotypes of French quality and cheap, quickly produced British goods.

Planning for the future of a supersonic transport before the 1962 treaty was also minimal, but more had been done in Britain than in France. The British conceived of two aircraft but aimed for the longer-range plane, which indeed proved potentially more marketable. The British, however, probably had gone further in such planning because of their engineering advantage, not because they had calculated with greater care a realistic market. The estimates for more than one thousand Concordes were reached merely by drawing lines between major cities more than one thousand and fewer than four thousand miles apart.

Neither the British nor the French succeeded in involving their own national airlines, let alone other international carriers, in the earliest planning. Concorde therefore never had a single willing customer. Manufacturers, and the political leaders who listened to them, believed that the airlines would be obliged to buy each new technological advance, whatever the purchase price and whatever the operational efficiency. Such an expectation had proved false for every previous British commercial aircraft development, but the manufacturers had this time found international partners and an unbreakable treaty between governments.

There was a pattern in the decisions not to cancel. Despite their different motives for entering into the treaty, for both British and French leaders the dominant concerns became employment, electoral consequences for key politicians, and competition with the United States. Neither commercial criteria nor planning projections were ever decisive in either country. Governments in both countries felt the pressures of unions and industry far more than the warning signals flashed early by their own airline planners.

British and French leaders shared a vision for Concorde. This European plane would prove that it was possible to compete with the United States in high technology. They would create jobs, win great prestige as technological pioneers, and eventually reap substantial profits from international sales.

These same leaders shared strategies aimed at the achievement of this vision. They relied on the judgments and advice of manufacturers and the encouragement of defense advisers. They neglected planning for the product. They dismissed environmental concerns, although the

British later took environmental issues more seriously. They went through periods of stinginess and extravagance in contributing to Concorde's development, and each side at various times wanted to cancel or forced the partner to continue. The outcome may have been inglorious. It may have highlighted respective weaknesses. But the process also exposed highly similar visions, criteria for achievement, obsessions with production rather than marketing, and limitations on actors designed to assure narrow objectives. And the process revealed the distortions of conventional wisdom. The British were not cheaper than the French; the French did not forecast the future more accurately or plan more systematically. Technocrats could control costly decisions in Britain as much as in France, and politicians in France could be as susceptible to bread-and-butter issues as politicians in Britain. For both the French and the British, Concorde produced a common U.S. villain and no native heroes. It proved that Britain and France were capable of great joint achievement (they did build and fly Concorde), and of great collaborative folly. They could equal each other's genius, creativity, inefficiency, incompetence, tragedy, and waste.

5

Political instability and high technology

It is possible to integrate the British and French stories of Concorde because they are so much alike. Despite popular impressions – that the ingenuity behind the plane was French, that the British alone wanted to cancel, that the British tried to build cheaply, that the French alone appreciated the plane's commercial potential, that the British were less vigorous than the French in penetrating the U.S. market – the British and the French agreed far more than they disagreed, especially on crucial decisions. Nevertheless, the common outcome from a joint enterprise must be contrasted with the different outcomes of separate ventures. As it is necessary to explain the causes for similar Concorde stories, so it is necessary to explain the different outcomes in the airport cases.

The joint development of supersonic transport organized by the British and French governments extends an impression of similarity between the two countries, but French observers have interpreted Concorde as typically French, both in its technical achievement and in its commercial failure. British observers have seen Concorde as typically British, although more for the squandering of technical advantage and national resources than for any technical accomplishment.

The recourse to cultural type is even more apparent in the airport cases, where superficial consideration sustains the conventional view that Britain and France are differ-

ent politically and culturally. The French built a new international airport while the British failed to do so. Yet most
features of these cases highlight similarities – in the priorities and values of the central decision makers; in efforts
to accomplish like objectives; in the designs, plans, and criteria of the projects. What is different is the result, and
traditional comparisons between Britain and France do not
restrict differences so narrowly. In combination with the
tale of Concorde, these cases suggest that similarities dominate differences between Britain and France, at least in
their management of high technology.

Concorde was a totally joint project, despite the implications of a Renault advertising campaign in the United
States in early 1982 and President Mitterrand's public pro-
nouncements during a subsequent U.S. visit, which seemed
to claim the technology as both pathbreaking and French.
When manufacturers across the Channel from each other
could not integrate their assembly lines, parallel production was established. Each country built approximately half
of the plane and paid half the bills (see Fig. 5.1). National
leaders obstinately disagreed for five years on the spelling
of the plane's name, yet Anthony Wedgwood Benn – no
Europeanist he – adopted the French version (with an "e")
on behalf of European cooperation. Although the failure
to integrate often has been attributed to irreconcilable national differences,[1] we shall see that alternative explanations are available.

Although differences appear narrow, they are present.
If Britain and France have similar priorities and strategies,
which discount the influence of different cultures and politics, then accomplishments ought also to be similar. The
airport cases deny this hypothesis, and some critics of Concorde think the plane's commercial failure more important than its simple realization, focusing their criticism on
the cultural peculiarities of the British and the French.
Hence alternative explanations must be offered for the inconsistent results in these cases.

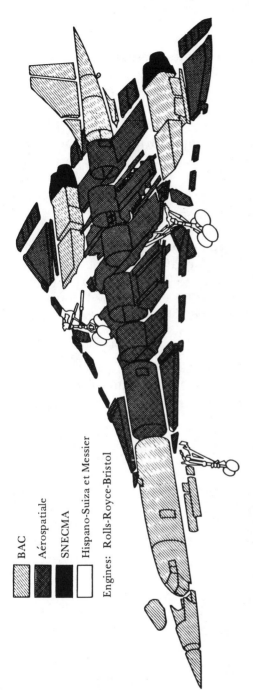

BAC

Aérospatiale

SNECMA

Hispano-Suiza et Messier

Engines: Rolls-Royce-Bristol

Figure 5.1. Concorde: apportionment of construction. Reprinted by permission of the publisher from Aviation International, no. 672, December 15–31, 1975, p. 39.

A second problem posed by these cases is their possible peculiarity. Are they cases *of* anything? Robert Gilpin, of course, reported that the Gaullist strategy in science was to collaborate with other states on advanced technology projects for competition with the Americans, and he offered Concorde as an important example. British behavior, however, requires a separate explanation, and the airport cases may appear detached from international relations and therefore not examples of this Gaullist approach. It is important to understand, consequently, that these cases were not unique to either country.

A third problem concerns criteria for judgment. The French built both a new airport and Concorde. Did they not succeed? The British failed to build a new airport and, on at least one occasion, would have abandoned Concorde had the French not threatened a legal suit in the Hague. Did they not then fail in these cases? Do the outcomes, in the end, not sustain the stereotypes?

If all the cases are to be judged failures for quality, how ought decisions to have been made, and how should they be made in future? Should the French invite public participation? Should the British limit more such participation? Should the British concentrate authority, or the French disperse it? Would such changes improve the quality of decisions and outcomes?

Finally, the policies supporting the construction of civil aviation infrastructure and Concorde had lasting consequences for the economies, transport systems, and research and development strategies of both Britain and France. A policy analysis must note the lasting distortions created by these projects.

COMPARE OR CONTRAST

Differences

The survey evidence that emphasizes differences in values held by European élites of different nations illustrates well the consequent differences in political institutions.[2] However, this literature does not confront the values animating specific behavior under similar conditions. The French may seem to value egalitarianism and the British may seem to prefer liberalism, but decision makers of both nationalities in the cases studied here sought essentially the same objectives, even if they did not always achieve them. Even if the original objectives were different, as with Concorde, over the course of these projects the responsible officials set the same priorities, utilized the same criteria, and even mapped the same strategies. Differences in their values (the heart of a cultural explanation) therefore cannot explain different outcomes, and the story of Concorde helps to arrest the inclination to weight cultural contrasts in understanding British and French performance.

Other differences prove more apparent than real. The British appeared the more cost-conscious during Concorde's development, but it was the French who refused to spend more for design changes in 1974. British institutions exposed a continuing agony over costs, whereas similar worries in France were kept systematically from public view. Thus it is not possible to conclude that the British monitored cost more closely than the French; it is possible only to observe that British institutions promoted public exposure of financial misgivings.

French officials most concerned about the potential for marketing Concorde were more effectively ignored than their British counterparts, but they nevertheless were present, beginning with the 1960 engineer's report prepared at Air France. The French deflected or ignored criticism in building both Charles de Gaulle Airport and Concorde, whereas the plane and the third London airport involved continuous public debate in Britain. Still, British officials of both major political parties managed to hold off the opponents of Concorde, and the British, too, were capable of secrecy – as they proved in the "secret inquiry within government" reviewing the Chelmsford Inquiry inspector's report.[3] In France, institutional arrangements and popular support for prestige projects tended to channel criticism away from the political arena, endowing French officials with supreme self-confidence[4] because they believed in their projects (as did the British), and they believed they would be honored for their work (something their British counterparts frequently doubted). They also feared public debate, however, and therefore often refused to release "technical" information because laymen, French technocrats asserted, could not understand it. Other experts sometimes disrupted French technical assertions; in the example of estimating airport capacity, even for another country, the British experts certainly appear more accurate than the French. This difference arises, moreover, because British planners have been more creative, using pricing mechanisms to distribute traffic over a full day for a reduction in peak hour (and peak season) congestion.

The most apparent contrast in British and French approaches came in dealing with the Americans over access to New York for Concorde. But here, as in other examples of contrast, the impression created by style cannot outweigh the realities of substance. The British and the French had the same objectives and complemented each other in their strategies. The British seemed to have more faith in American democratic institutions, which would entitle foreign countries to equal legal status with Americans and their institutions, whereas the French seemed to place more trust in political negotiations between heads of state. Hence, ironically, the approaches to the U.S. problem tended to contradict the central political values commonly associated with British and French political cultures, for the British might have preferred the pluralist methods of bargaining and negotiation among élites that characterized Anglo-American relations more generally,[5] and the French might have supported greater faith in expressions of a general will through formality and law.

The differences in British and French thinking, especially over marketing Concorde, should not be underestimated, but they also should not be exaggerated. Because they reflect the organizational structure of each country's domestic politics, they do suggest contrasts in political values. However, this reflection often is inconsistent with the popular cultural images.

Similarities

David Henderson and François de Closets have indicted their respective countries for the failures of Concorde.[6] Each criticizes the peculiarly British or the peculiarly French styles, values, strategies, and procedures. Yet the objections they raise are essentially interchangeable, so that no sense of national peculiarity remains when they are compared. Their three central criticisms are of (1) the anonymity of the decision makers, (2) the secrecy in which they worked, and (3) the use of a cloak of national security to protect a theoretically military project from oversight. French civil servants, for example, refused to provide deputies in the National Assembly accurate information on costs,[7] and until Anthony Wedgwood Benn's 1967 revelations to the House of Commons, the British were systematically kept from knowledge of the extent of cost overruns. Henderson and de Closets conclude, contrary to the popular view, that Concorde diminished the prestige of their respective countries.

Because Concorde's development came under military supervision in both Britain and France, it was not subjected to serious commercial evaluation. Special budgets were put at the military's disposal. The design changes influenced by the airlines did not include worries about cost recovery. Furthermore, the national priority accorded the project, in both cases because the aircraft industry was the most prestigious and most strategically sensitive sector, made both governments dependent on the manufacturers. Julian Amery reported with satisfaction that by the time the treaty was signed the British Government and the manufacturers spoke with one voice,[8] and the corresponding French industry, nationalized in 1936, usually charted policy and already spoke for the government. One telling example of the intimacy of government and the manufacturers is the transition of Lord Beswick, from 1970 to 1974 special adviser to the chairman of BAC, to the position of minister of state for aviation in the Department of Industry. Jean-Pierre Mithois complained in *Le Figaro* on February 6, 1974: "The excessively optimistic forecasts were the fault of the public authorities who listened, if not complacently then passively, to the assurances of the aircraft industry."

Both the French and the British had ample warning of the commercial risks, and both governments chose to continue. The differences were more of degree than of perspective. Raymond Nivet, comparing British manufacturing predictions in 1969 (minimum sale of 250 and maximum of 1,250 by 1978) to a 1961 French expectation (at least 385 Concordes by 1975, including 185 on French domestic routes), characterized the difference as "typical British understatement."[9]

Political Left and Right, in both Britain and France, supported these prestige projects, even though emphasis on a French Communist Party has led many observers to evoke contrasts in the British and French political spectra. In all cases the Right invoked the prestige and the Left spoke of jobs. The irony, of course, was that the Left actively supported major public expenditure for élitist, exclusive, luxury projects. When the Right seemed ready to give up on the third London airport, the Labour Party proposed the four-runway development of Stansted, and when the Conservatives proposed the elaborate Maplin Sands solution, the Left ordered cancellation. When Georges Pompidou expressed doubts about Concorde, it was Georges Marchais, invoking union support, who demanded continuation; when the Gaullist Right wanted the installation of the *aérotrain*, it was Jacques Chaban-Delmas who refused. In the waning years of the Concorde project, its two most prominent defenders were Marchais and Benn. Neither domestic political stripe nor national flag defined the disagreements reliably.

Both the British and the French exaggerated what technological development could do for their international status and their respective economies. Both believed additional aviation infrastructure with the latest technology to be essential for their trade, and they believed equally that Concorde was vital to their industries. Both believed that technology was the key to successful competition with each other (both alerted their countrymen to the threat of airport development across the Channel), and they believed together that technological advance would let them retain economic independence from the United States. This latter concern, perhaps more formidable for the French, emerged as the principal common objective for Concorde.

This belief in technology was premised on a common value placed on competition and a national or European independence from the United States. As proud countries they could each rally to a national accomplishment, but the same values found pride in the same accomplishments. Here again, chauvinism was not reserved for the political Right. The Left cited patriotism as well as jobs to defend Concorde. Georges Marchais insisted, "We shouldn't give in to American pressure,"[10] although part of his solution was a threat to collaborate with the Soviet Union.

Governments in both Britain and France imposed Concorde on their national airlines, neither of which wanted to buy or operate the plane. Both governments had to subsidize the purchase and the operations. And both had to salvage the industries that suffered through nationalizations, mergers, and consolidations associated with the achievement of government objectives.

Despite the remarkable support for these costly high technology projects, and the general tendency to reject social, economic, or environmental concerns, governments in both Britain and France proved themselves on occasion sensitive to public criticism. The British rejection of various sites for the third London airport came repeatedly on social and economic, not technical, grounds, and although there were technological doubts, Chaban-Delmas's repudiation of the *aérotrain* was above all a social and political choice. Again, there may be differences of degree or frequency between Britain and France, but important examples of similar behavior are abundant.

Most observers detected far more public participation in Britain than in France. It is apparent that Concorde and Charles de Gaulle Airport had their critics and that with rare exception they scarcely penetrated the French media or public conscience. There may be many more voluntary programs and societies in Britain than in France, for well-documented reasons, but it does not follow that the French are more docile or socially unconscious because the media pay them less attention or their formal organizations are fewer. Jack Hayward may have deplored British tripartism and preferred the "interlocking economic directorate" he had observed in France,[11] but he also may not have been enamored of the comparable directorate that governed Britain's commitment to Concorde. British protesters and critics, in achieving periodic project delays of the third London airport, have been more successful than their French counterparts, but for largely institutional reasons.

EXPLANATIONS

Conventional interpretations

Institutional, not cultural, differences are the key to understanding the differences in outcome over airport development and the similarity of failure over Concorde. There may be cultural explanations for the differences in media treatment, for example, but media performance was no more central to outcomes than public participation.

There may be cultural and political roots to the institutions (as in the presence or absence of public hearings), but such an explanation is of a different order from one attributing élite behavior on a common problem to cultural differences. In these cases, common cultural preferences have been processed by different institutions, which has led sometimes to different results.

The misunderstanding of Britain and France can be seen in the conventional wisdom that has interpreted these cases in the past. Despite the view promoted in France, there is no mistaking the development of Charles de Gaulle Airport for the *cohérence* praised by Shonfield, even though the facility easily satisfies his criteria for investments that require long lead times.[12] Nor does Charles de Gaulle Airport meet Pierre Massé's criteria of merit for the National Plan: "to reduce, thanks to better coordination of policies, overlapping and spare capacities."[13] Charles de Gaulle did precisely the opposite. Yet the airport has been offered as the symbol of French achievement in both rational central planning and high technology.

Of course, France fared no better than Britain on Concorde, and if all is not what it seems to be in French "success," the sources of British "failure" have not been identified more reliably. Excessive participation was not the source of defeat for the third London airport, any more than it could be held accountable for assuring the construction of Concorde; and the influence of perceived union preferences was present in both countries.[14]

The suggestion that French success was attributable to superior decision makers is contradicted in all these cases. The assumptions and conclusions of the Roskill Commission may be disputed technically and analytically, but no study for civil aviation infrastructure in France demonstrated any comparable care, calculation, or expertise, and throughout Concorde's history British critics of cost and noise were more numerous and more accurate than the French. British aviation forecasting, although not remarkable, was more sophisticated and more accurate than the French, and it played a greater role in decision making.[15] Furthermore, the quest for more expertise in British government assumes that experts will agree on the best solutions to problems. The evidence in all these cases shows that experts disagree in accordance with their clients. Airline specialists rejected both the new airports and Concorde, whereas partisans of the manufacturers offered confident marketing forecasts for Concorde and airport authorities predicted certain saturation of their facilities. The character of advice may appear more partisan in France, but primarily because of the location of expertise in the political system. *Flight International* commented, in view of these arrangements: "Senior French aircraft engineers are beginning to talk of how much they envy the British their amateur civil servants, who usually listen to and consult industry before making policy decisions. The élite, aeronautically trained French civil servants appear to some sections of middle management in French industry to be too inbred and know-it-all."[16] These remarks were cited, moreover, when French manufacturers were having their way over Concorde.

However much the French civil servant may know, decision making structures do not necessarily produce rational choices. French technocrats may have more power than the British, but the consequence is not necessarily "better" outcomes. Neither Charles de Gaulle Airport nor Concorde is a monument to rationality, and other examples abound. The advertising twin in the Renault–Concorde campaign was a sequence showing off "the world's fastest train." The TGV (*train de grande vitesse,* later called *trés grande vitesse*) races between Paris and Lyon, and whatever its technical merits, its application has been political and bears brief review here.

When Aéroport de Paris built Charles de Gaulle Airport at Roissy, the powerful mayor of Lyon demanded and got government help to build another new international airport, Lyon–Satolas. Recent National Plans had argued that, in addition to the undesirable concentration of economic activity in the Paris basin, France was suffering from disproportionate development east of a line running diagonally from Le Havre to Marseilles. The National Plans called for improvements in infrastructure west of the line to encourage investment and industry. Yet a first major response was the formation of the best intercity air system in France to serve the two major cities, Paris and Lyon, east of the line.

The second major response was the TGV. Burned by the construction of Lyon–Satolas and initially spurned by Aéroport de Paris as a provider of transit to Charles de Gaulle, the SNCF lobbied successfully for the financial subsidy necessary to develop and implement the newest rail technology. The TGV would be built, however, where it would best serve the rail corporation, on the most heavily traveled route in France. So instead of pursuing a rational approach to France's developmental imbalance, the government thrice awarded to the most developed areas the newest, most expensive technologies – the airport, the TGV, and the newly completed autoroute – thereby reinforcing the very tendencies deplored in the National Plans. The results might have been rational economically (serving established markets), but they were not produced by French planning. The British High Speed Train, moreover, escaped such planning contradictions because it did not compete directly with the best alternative infrastructure.

Although it is possible to emphasize French irrationality to challenge one conventional wisdom, it is also possible to discover British abuse of power to challenge another. When convenient, British authorities behaved no more responsibly or democratically than the French. A telling example may be found in the testing of Concorde. Like the French, the British tried to manage the media (and with comparable success, with the *Observer* reduced in Britain to a role similar to that of the *Canard Enchaîné* in France); proving flights conducted away from populated areas were declared as evidence that Concorde would not be disturbing, and concern about the sonic boom was dismissed. The chauvinism of the French was manifested as patriotism by the British, and public criticism of the national enterprise was met by the same official scorn in Britain as it had encountered in France.

French cynicism was more effective politically, and the French approach to the application of high technology does imply the corruption of power. However, there is more that needs to be said about how the French political system made such corruption possible. The conventional explanation of centralized and concentrated power obviously fails in the Charles de Gaulle case because of the uncoordinated efforts of central authorities.

Unconventional interpretations

The values that dictated building major aviation infrastructure and the world's most sophisticated aircraft were shared by British and French élites. They stipulated the same criteria, with the same priorities. Hochmuth, however, traces Concorde's failures to fundamental differences between the two countries when the 1962 treaty was signed: "Analysis of the detailed program shows that the product-market goals of the British and the French sides were still as far apart as ever. What they had agreed to was a common means to achieve their separate goals and to share the total expenses and ultimate profits."[17] Yet within a year the separate goals of long-range and medium-range planes designed for different routes and customers had been merged into a single design and a common objective. Whatever the cultural and organizational differences,[18] the desire to best the Americans by means of a marketable long-range supersonic transport prevailed.

Hochmuth's analysis of Concorde's development failure

is more persuasive if we consider an alternative deployment of his own industrial organization data. One of the central problems of building Concorde derived from the need to integrate the activities of separate manufacturing corporations. Barriers of language, tradition, and geography noted by Hochmuth compounded the inevitable problems of different organizations working together, but Concorde's difficulties derived more from the challenges of corporate merger than from the differences between nation-states.

Manufacturing instability. The engine and airframe manufacturers probably disagreed with each other as much within Britain and France as they did across the Channel. The Olympus engine was designed by Bristol-Siddeley, and in accordance with the treaty designating French leadership for engine development, the British plans were absorbed by SNECMA, the French manufacturer. But leadership on the airframe was more difficult because both British and French firms had advanced designs early in the planning.

Problems over the engines arose for three reasons. First, the technology dated from the 1950s and could not meet evolving technical requirements. Second, the plane was designed around the engines, which prevented radical changes on the whole aircraft when they were apparently needed. Third, in a transaction engineered by Minister for Technology Anthony Wedgwood Benn, Bristol-Siddeley, already the product of a 1959 merger involving six companies, was taken over by Rolls Royce in 1966. Rolls Royce, soon burdened with other major projects (including the RB 211 for Lockheed's TriStar L1011, also negotiated by Benn), was ill equipped to integrate Concorde. As organizational instability set in on the British side, the French manufacturer grew anxious and irritated.

The airframe conflicts were more serious, especially because these firms assumed overall design leadership for the plane. In the 1959 reorganization that left only two engine manufacturers in Britain, only two British airframe manufacturers survived, Hawker-Siddeley and a conglomerate of four companies, now called the British Aircraft Corporation (BAC). One component of BAC, Bristol Aircraft Corporation, had launched the work on the Concorde, but only after winning a pretreaty design competition with Hawker-Siddeley. On the French side, the main airframe design came from Sud Aviation, itself the product of a merger in the late 1950s.

BAC and Sud Aviation each thought itself superior to the partner. Each, therefore, was reluctant to accept any leadership but its own. Integrated management through committees with rotating chairmen was meant to force the marriage, but there was perpetual conflict. Furthermore, and probably more important, the chairman of BAC faced competing demands from four submerged companies, three of which disputed the priority accorded Concorde. TSR-2, the VC 10, and the BAC 111 were all now under the umbrella firm that was also producing Concorde, and all therefore required attention from the same supervising management. This was an intractable, internal management problem within the British corporation.

Appearances on the French side may have been of a single corporation speaking for the government,[19] but the leadership of Sud Aviation was not always in corporate and project control. The presidency of Sud was changed by the government three times within six years of treaty signing, and the second replacement named by the government was the prefect of the Paris police, hardly a technical or aviation paragon. The Concorde team leader, Jean Forestier, resigned in frustration in 1968, and his designated successor refused the job. Two years later Sud Aviation was merged into Aérospatiale with two other companies, and the Concorde team was soon reduced in relative size and importance.

During the period of Concorde's development the aircraft manufacturing industry in both Britain and France was undergoing an organizational revolution. Technical leadership was in flux as corporate mergers placed Concorde in competition for management attention with other projects of sister companies. In September 1967 Britain and France joined Germany in an agreement to build a European wide-body, the Airbus. BAC believed the plane vital to its own future, but Benn insisted that engine leadership be delivered to Rolls Royce as a condition of British participation. Rolls Royce, already straining from its obligations on Concorde and to Lockheed, would subsequently be forced to abandon Airbus, thus severing the original British connection and BAC's immediate future in the wide-body business. The French, meanwhile, were adding equally to established burdens and management confusion. Since neither country could get its corporate house in order, these efforts to force a transnational marriage only complicated a deteriorating industry.

In Hochmuth's account there is no evidence that Anglo-French discord was of a different kind, or had a different effect on the Concorde project, than the pains of merger and management within the corporate structures of each country. The refusal to surrender design leadership by Sud Aviation and BAC was typical of corporations who marry reluctantly, their national characteristics notwithstanding.

These managerial and technical problems delayed delivery but did not prevent development of Concorde. With the frictions and finances exacerbated by the events of 1968, the international treaty and subsequent government-to-government undertakings may have been the only reasons the corporate partners did not give up. They were obliged to sublimate their differences in style and to maximize their agreement on goals and technique. As Frank Melville wrote in *Fortune,* Concorde may "ha[ve] to be viewed as a triumph of politics and national pride over managerial common sense,"[20] but there were two nations sharing both the politics and the pride.

Government instability. I argued in Chapter 3 that plans for the third London airport fell victim primarily to government instability. This instability was defined by alternations in power of two political parties with contradictory concepts of the organization of government, and by the frequent reassignment of responsibility for projects requiring interdepartmental cooperation to new experts with differing criteria for planning and assessment. The airport portfolio was transferred repeatedly among ministries and departments, and each government change was accompanied by new evaluative criteria and new supervisory personnel. A project that began as a service to anticipated air passengers was remanded to trade analysts responsible for maximizing operational profit, especially from foreign sources, and eventually to an environmental department trying to integrate disparate concerns within the airport plans. Over this period technology also changed, shifting calculated needs from runways to terminals and confounding logical site selection. Frequent electoral reversals made each new design politically vulnerable.

This analysis raises two questions. First, the electoral and ministerial changes that derailed the airport plans did not ground Concorde. Why not? Second, there also was considerable government instability in France during this period, the popular image of the Fifth Republic notwithstanding. For example, the responsible minister of transport changed three times during six months of the treaty negotiations, and organizational location of the aviation portfolio moved formally seven times in little more than a decade. Why did this organizational and personnel turbulence not have the same effects in France as in Britain?

There are two main answers to these questions, one associated with the peculiarities of a particular project and the other identifying the impact of like symptoms on different systems. The character of a project obviously influences its probable achievement because of the number of actors and competing (or potentially cooperating) agencies that must be involved. Concorde was to be built by four manufacturers in their own factories. It created jobs with government money, but until the prototype could fly it involved no competing or sectoral interests. Environmental and ecological concerns could be deferred as speculative until the plane was built, and treasury controls could be suspended because of military supervision. Although technological and environmental consequences were unknown, objectives and perceived requirements were constant. Disagreement among the actors could not be misinterpreted as dissension because the general public knew neither the narrowness of the interests nor the costs they incurred. The consequence of political instability, then, even in Britain, was to deprive a project confined to two domestic corporations protected by military secrecy of close political review. Portfolio transfer did not alter the narrow mandate of the corporations, and no minister was in place long enough to gain control of the corporations (see Table 5.1). Moreover, fear of treaty violation invoked only two years after signing discouraged later political interference. The *Economist* observed, when Benn exposed escalating costs to the House of Commons in 1974: "The ministers in charge of Concorde, from its formative years in 1958 to the present time, have changed so rapidly that none of them was in office long enough to form an opinion of his own about the quality of advice being given."[21] The advice being given, of course, came primarily from the manufacturers, supported by the military. When British Airways periodically renewed its discomfort over the project, the manufacturers complained that the flag carrier already had proven itself unpatriotic, even disloyal, by criticizing the VC 10.

Unlike the third London airport, which required the coordination of agencies with complementary responsibilities, Concorde was supervised by a continuous coterie of civil servants who had a single responsibility and whose political leadership kept changing. During the very summer of the treaty negotiation Macmillan dispatched half

Table 5.1. *British ministerial changes and Concorde*

Date	Responsible minister	Title
1958	Aubrey Jones	Minister of Supply
1959	Duncan Sandys	Minister of Aviation
1960	Peter Thorneycroft	Minister of Aviation
1962	Julian Amery	Minister of Aviation
1964	Roy Jenkins	Minister of Aviation
1965	Fred Mulley	Minister of Aviation
1967	Anthony Wedgwood Benn	Minister of Technology
1970	Geoffrey Rippon	Minister of Technology
	John Davies	Secretary of State for Trade and Industry
	Frederick Corfield	Minister of Aviation Supply; then Minister for Aerospace
1972	Michael Heseltine	Minister for Aerospace
	Peter Walker	Secretary of State for Trade and Industry
1974	Anthony Wedgwood Benn	Secretary of State for Industry
1976	Eric Varley	Secretary of State for Industry
	Roy Mason	Secretary of State for Defence
1977	Fred Mulley	Secretary of State for Defence
1980	Sir Keith Joseph	Secretary of State for Industry
	Francis Pym	Secretary of State for Defence
1981	Patrick Jenkin	Secretary of State for Trade and Industry
	John Nott	Secretary of State for Defence
1983	Norman Tebbitt	Secretary of State for Trade and Industry
	Michael Heseltine	Secretary of State for Defence
	Nicholas Ridley	Secretary of State for Transport

his cabinet; Amery himself was new to the job. However, the mission was not redefined when cabinets changed or the portfolio moved because the responsible subordinate team remained intact. When Trade and Industry were merged by a Conservative Government into a single department, marketing advice simply came from the manufacturers and their supporters. The narrowness of the mission, the essential control of the manufacturers, and the continuity of the civil servants (who accepted the primacy of engineering expertise) differentiated the Concorde experience from that of the third London airport.

The obligations of the international treaty combined with the dimensions of domestic instability to keep political oversight minimal. Such instability, and the influence of the treaty, had similar effects in France, minimizing control even more. The British system, despite these factors, did remain responsive. When the Government changed, Concorde was subjected to serious review and political attempts to cancel. The treaty may have made life easier for Concorde, but the plane still did not have an easy ride in Britain's unstable political and economic conditions, and the treaty alone obviously did not save the plane.

The French tendency to reorganize government and change ministers, even without electoral change, was not unlike the British, but two main factors in the case of airport development made the consequences different. First, the continuity of the party in power helped assure consensus on major projects. More important, however, was the fundamental administrative continuity despite institutional reorganization. The formal *tutelle* for Aéroport de Paris shifted, for example, from a Ministry of Transport and Public Works to a Ministry of Equipment with a Transport secretariat, and then to a Ministry of State, but the Transport unit remained intact and the airport portfolio stayed within it (see Table 5.2). Aéroport de Paris's planning capabilities continued to dwarf its political controllers, just as the nationalized manufacturers, with direct presidential commitment, dictated the terms to nominally superior politicians. The frequent rotation of ministers only reinforced the advantages of the agency and the manufacturers, for politicians were even less able to gain control of projects in France than they were in Britain.

The central difference between Britain and France, then, was not in the presence of instability but rather in its impact on institutional arrangements and the policy process. French political and even organizational turbulence swirled around entrenched forces with secure mandates; British instability led to broad transfers of responsibility that prevented some projects, such as the third London airport, from being launched at all. The symptoms of problems therefore were the same, and their similarity undermines

Table 5.2. *French political turbulence and Concorde*

Date	Responsible minister[a]	Title[a]
1958	Robert Buron	Minister for Public Works and Transport
1962	Roger Dusseaulx	Minister for Public Works and Transport
	Marc Jacquet	Minister for Public Works and Transport
1966	Edgard Pisani	Minister of Equipment
	André Bettencourt	Secretary of State for Transport
1967	Jean Chamant	Minister of Transport
1969	Raymond Mondon	Minister of Transport
1971	Jean Chamant	Minister of Transport
1972	Robert Galley	Minister of Transport
1973	Yves Guéna	Minister of Transport
1974	Olivier Guichard	Minister of State in the Ministry of Territorial Management, Equipment, and Transport
	Marcel Cavaillé	Secretary of State for Transport
1975	Norbert Ségard	Minister for Foreign Commerce
	Marcel Cavaillé	Secretary of State for Transport
1976	Raymond Barre	Minister for Foreign Commerce
	Marcel Cavaillé	Secretary of State for Transport
	Jean-Pierre Fourcade	Minister of Equipment
	Marcel Cavaillé	Secretary of State to the Minister of Equipment for Transport
1978	Jöel Le Theule	Minister of Transport
1980	Daniel Hoeffel	Minister of Transport
1981	Louis Mermax	Minister of Transport
1981–	Charles Fiterman	Minister of Transport

[a] Indentations indicate subordinate status with direct responsibility for Concorde.

any significance that might be attributed to different social values; but the consequences in different political structures were very different indeed.

UNIQUENESS

These cases are not isolated or unique either to Britain or France. There are comparable examples within aviation and in other sectors.[22] The Maplin project is already considered widely as typically British, albeit, as we have seen, for the wrong reasons. The Lyon–Satolas development, producing an inefficient two-airport system for Lyon, is very similar to the incoherent planning and politics of Charles de Gaulle Airport, and the third London airport saga echoes a series of misbegotten British public works, including the chunnel. Roissy-Rail is a case involving another state enterprise within the airport story, and problems of transportation on the Paris quays and in motorway construction generally are legends of their own in France. Incoherent French central planning is recognizable in the new towns program, in which the bill of particulars includes conflicts over radial versus circumferential roads, the absence of calculated trade-offs between public and private sector transport systems, and the absence of universities in any of the new communities. The conclusion indicts the lack of reliable coordinating mechanisms for the competing central agencies.[23] The projects discussed in this book were deemed vital to the development and prestige of crucial economic sectors by the governments involved; they were grander in scope and expense than many others that might be cited. Errors therefore are all the more glaring, for in these cases the governments performed at their very best.

Although this analysis does not embrace projects or policies outside transportation and civil aviation, it is notable that the pattern of instability associated with government reorganization has cut through all British and French departments during the past two decades. No fewer than fifty-nine major departments or ministries were transformed in Britain, whether through merger, relocation in the political system, or dismemberment, between 1963 and 1979. These changes do not include state enterprises that often absorbed responsibilities previously situated within government departments, such as airport operations, now in the British Airports Authority, or air safety, now in the Civil Aviation Authority. Not only was the airport portfolio divided, redivided, merged, and absorbed by a Ministry of Supply, Ministry of Aviation, Board of Trade, Department of Trade, Department of Trade and Industry, Department of the Environment, and Department of Transport; the aircraft portfolio for Concorde was shifted through Supply, Aviation, Technology, Trade and Industry, Aerospace, Defence, and Industry. Science issues wandered over time from jurisdictions in Education, Scientific and Industrial Research, and Technology; and a similar report can be rendered on numerous other government activities ranging from employment services to welfare and health care. Some of these changes were in name only, but even when whole units remained intact the agenda of their political masters – with an ever-changing mix of components – could alter missions and disrupt continuity. Other British failures or government weaknesses during the postwar years may be better understood in light of this turbulence.

JUDGING PROCESSES AND RESULTS

Public policies must be assessed on at least two levels.[24] The first is determined by policy makers. They set goals and objectives for themselves, and they must be judged according to whether those goals and objectives are achieved. The second is more abstract. A housing authority may promise and subsequently build a specific number of units, but the policy should be judged on the social and economic quality of the units, as well as on the simple numerical standard. Similarly, an authority may propose and build an airport, but that accomplishment alone cannot guarantee a positive evaluation.

The three cases studied here are failures both by the criteria stipulated by policy makers and by more abstract criteria. Let us consider each one briefly according to these two analytical levels.

Charles de Gaulle Airport

French officials in the late 1950s set three main goals when a new airport north of Paris became the objective, the vehicle for goal accomplishment. Le Bourget Airport was to be closed, a move that would extend a greenbelt around Paris. All air traffic demand for the Paris region was to be accommodated into the twenty-first century. And lastly, aviation facilities in Paris were to glorify France as symbols of technological achievement. Later, still during the planning phases of the new airport, the National Plans designated the region in which the airport was to be located as free of commercial development so that economic growth could be channeled toward new towns.

The objective, the construction of a new airport north of Paris, was accomplished. Le Bourget Airport, however, was not closed. Commercial flights ceased, some twenty years after the initial planning, but general aviation and some charter traffic continued to operate through Le Bourget twenty-five years after the director of the Paris District had agreed with Aéroport de Paris on the need for a replacement airport. Moreover, the new airport itself deliberately violated the goals of the National Plans by using its state expropriation and fiscal powers to develop a commercial center.

All air traffic demand can be accommodated easily within the capacities of the Paris airports, but inadequate surface access and incoherent traffic distribution between facilities may have helped reduce demand. Finally, the technological innovations of the new airport are flawed. The construction of a new airport was an objective meant to satisfy other goals, but accomplishment of the objective did not assure satisfaction of those goals.

Charles de Gaulle Airport's more abstract deficiencies are considerable. Its construction exacted significant social as well as economic cost. The real estate market north of Paris became inflated. Roissy-Rail was built on a costly schedule and in an inefficient location. Airline clients were unhappy with the new expenses imposed on them by the facility's design. A community, Roissy-en-France, was destroyed, and other deceived neighbors began to suffer unanticipated noise. It is impossible to weigh these costs systematically against the advantages of guaranteed traffic capacity because they represent competing values. But it is possible to wonder whether responsible decision makers, had they known of the social costs before building, would have made the same commitments. That they did not know was in significant measure a consequence of the organization of political institutions and the structure of the decision process.

The third London airport

British officials set the same objectives as the French, although not in service of identical goals. The British were not reclaiming an airport or assuring green space, but they were seeking to guarantee airport capacity into the twenty-first century.

Initial British planning was narrowly focused on the objective of airport construction to meet projected traffic demand. Several development proposals were promoted in accordance with the interests of aviation enthusiasts. However, British goals throughout the planning period kept changing. Emphasis was given variously to port facilities for the island nation, environmental protection, respect for historical sites and monuments (an important calculation of the Roskill Commission), trade and tourist promotion, employment, and budget balancing. As the goals changed, commitment to the objective wavered, and often the objective was thought incompatible with the goals.

Political instability gave different goals the opportunity to dominate at different times. The narrow airport construction objective was the victim. Yet the key aviation goal, to meet traffic demand, was met by more creative use of existing facilities and land. It was not that the British failed to act but rather that they were forced to be imaginative with more modest ventures than the construction of a new airport. Moreover, the numerous planning exercises must be recognized as actions that warned against still greater action of a different kind. The British were guilty not of doing nothing but rather of changing their minds repeatedly about what they wanted to do and where it was to be done. The bolder French initiative obscured lesser, but perhaps more effective, alternatives that the British eventually discovered. Hence, as efforts to accomplish the British objective – building a third London airport – failed, British goals generally were met. There was considerable waste of money and manpower on plans and studies for the construction of a facility never built, but goals were met at far less expense than would have been exacted through accomplishment of the objective.

The failure to build spared Britain incalculable costs. No land was purchased or expropriated from private owners. Air traffic did grow, although not at all at the pace projected in the 1950s and 1960s. New facilities were built – especially terminals and surface transit and parking systems – at Heathrow, Gatwick, and Luton. Such incremental growth undoubtedly increased pressure on established infrastructure and exposed more people to more constant noise. Yet during the quarter century of commercial jet aviation there has been a steady reduction in the noise from new engines, and no large Greater London populations unaccustomed to aircraft noise have been subjected to it by new infrastructure. The British failure to build a whole new airport spared the public most social cost and considerable capital investment; it minimized harm while meeting broad policy goals.

The British airport outcome demonstrated that major capital investment is not always required to maintain a competitive international position. The British failed to capture the hunted white elephant. They may yet require considerable ingenuity to meet traffic demand by the end of the century, but into the 1980s they could still argue that lumbering white elephants are not worth their feed.

Concorde

The joint commitment to Concorde exacted both measurable and social costs. The employment created by the project became a trap preventing cancellation. The technological frontier left the pioneers open to a free fall from space. The temporary advantages to the aircraft industry of watering at the public trough became a liability of overdependence on a single unsound commercial project. Long-term Anglo-French cooperation was not enhanced.

The initial goals for Concorde were met partially or not at all. Instead of besting the United States in aviation technology, the Europeans forfeited an apparent lead in other aircraft, notably the Airbus. Instead of reaping profit, they sustained the greatest losses in the history of the industry. Expected prestige was criticized as overbearing pride. Britain's entry into Europe took another decade, and Concorde was not a factor. Of all the goals, perhaps the one achieved was the technical advance made by the French industry. But the objective, building Concorde, surely became central enough to responsible officials for them to lose sight of the goals that originally had animated the enterprise.

Completion of a project, then – accomplishment of an objective – does not guarantee the satisfaction of goals for which the objective was chosen. This cardinal rule of planning theory is particularly salient in these cases. Judgment can be rendered according to the criteria enunciated by the decision makers themselves. In addition, social costs can be observed, not because a trade-off can be calculated but because a focus on the decision maker's criteria must not allow such costs to be ignored. In these cases, the social costs have been considerable, but the judgment of failure is dictated by the intentions of national leaders.

RELATED CONSEQUENCES

There are many practical consequences of these cases. French National Plans and the potential success of the new towns were compromised by Charles de Gaulle Airport and subsequently by the construction of Lyon–Satolas and the

TGV. The great investments in Charles de Gaulle Airport and Roissy-Rail converted a modestly efficient two-airport system into a grossly inefficient three-airport system in which all infrastructure except roads became underutilized. The Roskill Commission, the Maplin Development Authority, and numerous interdepartmental committees, reviews, white papers, and laws passed and repealed for a third London airport cost the British millions of pounds, decades of professional attention and expertise, and incalculable frustration and embarrassment.

Cooperative futures

Among politicians and aviation specialists it is assumed that the workers and managers of Filton and Toulouse became none the friendlier for the years of collaboration on Concorde. Each blamed the other for failure. Yet despite the disagreements over the fourteen years of active interchange, the plane was built amid substantial engineering pride. It is not enough, in failure, to conclude that collaboration did not serve a European cause. One must wonder whether, had the plane succeeded, the potential for an integrated European industry more capable of competing with the United States might have been enhanced.

Certainly the Concorde experience helped erode mutual stereotypes. British forecasts on Concorde's potential tended to be more accurate than the French, and they were introduced earlier and more often. The British were wiser and more successful in their strategy for gaining access to the United States. French industry may have improved far more than the British as a result of the whole process, but French experts gained a much greater respect for the competence of their British counterparts.

There was a poetic justice to the initial concepts of the Concorde, born in the French Fifth Republic and the Conservative Government that was fighting to salvage corners of the British Empire in Cyprus and Aden. The French scheme, for a medium-range plane, matched a perceived need to reach the last imperial outpost in Algiers. The British, with a more far-flung empire and more systematic notions of a commonwealth reaching farther still, appropriately projected a long-range plane. And it probably took erstwhile empires to encourage thinking in terms of supersonic transport at all. It is not surprising that the only countries to conceive producing such a plane were the United States, the USSR, Britain, and France, and that the most promising customer for the plane was the shah of Iran. In the early 1960s only these countries could even imagine competing with one another on the frontier of such large-scale innovative high technology.

For all the differences between Britain and France, then, they made far more progress on a supersonic transport than did a single U.S. firm not beset by corporate mergers or transnational agreements. The Anglo-French differences may have affected progress adversely, but in view of the U.S. and Soviet failures with comparable expenditures and commitments, these differences cannot be considered decisive. The willingness finally to agree to a single name for a project that had begun with four different models in itself testifies to the growing cooperation. Perhaps, in the end, the key lesson gained from Concorde was the ultimate accommodation possible on priorities and goals. Even as they failed, the British and French learned that they were not as unlike each other as they themselves might previously have supposed.

AN IDEAL POLICY PROCESS?

As the British and French came to understand each other more fully through cooperation over Concorde, they came to recognize similar impediments in their respective policy-making processes. The sources of failure in Britain and France were not always the same, even though the decision processes were more similar than commonly imagined. The

French were less rational and the British more professional than conventional wisdom would suggest, but there do remain certain significant elements of difference.

Control of the French process for development of a new airport was closed. A narrowly mandated agency dictated final site selection, construction schedules, facility design, traffic distribution. What the agency did not control did not get done, because coordination and cooperation with other responsible agencies barely existed. The overall success of the project required this sort of interagency activity, but nothing in the structure of French decision making guaranteed the integration of functions and roles.

French planning was nonparticipatory, both with respect to concerned citizens and private sector interests and with respect to implicated agencies of government. Because the task of airport development by definition required the participation of agencies with varying responsibilities, a nonparticipatory planning structure could be neither rational nor coherent. It could not embrace step-by-step choices accounting for all reasonably foreseeable contingencies because there was no systematic attempt to discover such contingencies. Aéroport de Paris planners were so confident of their expertise that they regarded outside comment as unwanted criticism.

The French manufacturers of Concorde may have been inclined to the secrecy and privacy enjoyed by Aéroport de Paris, but the international treaty forced consultation, and therefore criticism, upon them. Without the British, the French might well have built a small, medium-range supersonic transport that no one, including Air France, might ever have flown. One may also speculate that without the partnership neither country would have persisted in building Concorde, but the partnership did at least impose a modest sensitivity to the marketplace.

The reverence for French planning arose, of course, from the economic miracle of the 1950s and was transferred to grand public works. Yet a curiosity of the social science literature on this subject is its inability to prove any causal link between central planning and economic growth. Social science has no method for testing a nonexistent condition, so one can never know whether the French economy would have grown more or less with fewer central government functions. What social science can observe, however, is the temporary quality of the miracle and the limited conviction of politicians that central control and planning were an unqualified success. President Valéry Giscard d'Estaing, after long service as finance minister, was busy weakening central controls and encouraging private initiative because he believed that government influence was making the economy sag. President François Mitterrand's subsequent nationalizations did not instantly revitalize the French economy, and it did not take the Socialist president long to limit his own expectations about the capacity of the state.

Central planning, then, may not explain French economic success after World War II as much as Shonfield and others have argued. Such doubts imply that the failures in specific projects may be instructive for weaknesses in the overall planning process. And the principal source of these failures would seem to be narrow, nonparticipatory central control without comprehensive or coordinating authority. That source not only condemned Charles de Gaulle Airport; it also kept Concorde away from the warnings of fiscally responsible and cost-conscious officials.

The stereotype of *dirigisme* is supported by these observations, but only through a reversal of the traditional assessment of success and failure. The converse may be true in Britain. Although public hearings cannot be mistaken for participation (and many witnesses complained vigorously that such staged events were designed strictly to give the appearance of democracy),[25] competing values and criteria did gain access to the decision process and, through the cycle of structural change, did prevent construction of a third London airport. Participation did not yield this outcome, for changes were not the products of compromises struck by competitors meeting together. Rather, different views were introduced consecutively, each vetoing its predecessor. The British did not organize a decision process in which interested and implicated parties could negotiate (the traditional view notwithstanding), but unstable political institutions nevertheless assured that many different parties could be heard. Second thoughts were institutionalized, not to improve the quality of plans but to paralyze the realization of projects.

There can be no "ideal" decision or planning process because political systems and institutions are different and decisions and planning must be compatible with them. Nevertheless, there may be mutual lessons in the French and British experience. More information in advance of major capital expenditure plainly is preferable to less. The quantity of information available to decision makers expands with the number of interested parties contributing to discussion. Decisions cannot be made by all interested parties (a certain formula for paralysis), but appropriate information can be introduced.

There was deceit in the planning of Charles de Gaulle Airport, and in building and testing Concorde. This deceit did serve the objectives of project advocates eager to complete construction. However, it is not obvious that project advocates adequately represent the public interest. Had there been no cost deception over Concorde, the development might have been stopped mutually at an earlier stage, saving money and liberating the industry for more fruitful enterprise. Had the potential noise impact and projected land use of Charles de Gaulle Airport been known by the public, the project's scale might have been reduced (Delouvrier might not have supported the full land acquisition; the mayor of Goussainville and Communist deputies in the area might have dissented). A felicitous consequence might have been a limitation on subsequent overcapacity. It is not possible to stipulate which of these outcomes would have corresponded best to the public interest, but it is possible to suggest that the deception cast doubt on the enterprise's character as a public service.

SUMMARY AND CONCLUSION

Comparing public works

Most analyses by economists and political economists are not systematically comparative. They examine economic indicators and policies in specific industrial sectors, but not the process of setting and pursuing goals simultaneously in different political and economic systems. Airport construction, noted casually and symbolically as evidence of public investment, is not treated as a feature of "economic policy." It is, of course, such casual treatment of major public works that analytically compounds the error of policy makers, for huge capital investments in infrastructure may be the very essence of economic policy.

Postwar Anglo-French comparisons have centered on macroeconomic policy. These studies have emphasized differences between Britain and France by observing greater French economic success, and they have consistently given credit, as for the Italian economic miracle, to state central planning.[26] Early analyses by Vera Lutz, Stephen Cohen, Andrew Shonfield, and others focused on these differences in economic performance, and later assessments by Jack Hayward, Michael Watson, and others tended to confirm the observations but began to doubt the explanations. The causal linkage between planning and performance had been asserted but never demonstrated, and Hayward, Watson, and their coauthors argued that planning was a political, not a technical, process that served the status quo more than progress. Still, stereotypes about economic success prevailed, and cases were sectoral and nonspecific. Public works, even in studies of transportation sectors or construction industries, were paid little detailed attention.

When Peter Hall compared public works planning disasters in different countries, he sought to explain problems in the planning process, not differences or similarities in political systems.

The argument

Whatever might be observed broadly about Anglo-French cultural differences, the values held by élites making decisions for the high technology sector of civil aviation were essentially the same on both sides of the Channel. Both wanted to serve the traveling public, both wanted the biggest and best facilities in Europe, both wanted to outdo the United States, both wanted to be on the cutting edge of new technology. Both were prepared to marshal the resources of the state to serve these ends. Both were prepared to deceive their publics or to invoke secrecy to insulate themselves from public pressures. Both were prepared to spend more money than the private sector appeared ready to commit for grandiose projects. For all that may be said about Anglo-French misunderstanding, these élites understood each other well.

Failure stalked the projects chosen and pursued by both French and British élites, although superficially it appeared that the French had succeeded where the British had failed. The outcomes in two like cases were entirely different, a distinction that suggests contrast in values and institutions. Yet élite values were nearly identical, and the central institutional explanation for outcomes was also the same: Both French and British political systems suffered from political instability.

In both Britain and France ministers rarely retain portfolio responsibilities long enough to gain mastery over the subject or the bureaucracy. Both systems are prone to frequent ministerial rotation within governments, and the British through the 1960s and 1970s also alternated parties in power (a development new for the French, as yet with unknown consequences). Such frequent changes in political leadership assure greater authority for non-elected civil servants, who in both countries are highly skilled technocrats often devoted to state intervention for the resolution of problems.

This common institutional problem has led to very different consequences for the British and the French. Ministerial change in Britain normally is accompanied by institutional reorganization, especially but not exclusively when parties exchange power. Mandates and criteria for decision making therefore are in constant flux, with new teams of civil servants assigned to a problem, or old teams given new instructions and new interlocutors. The British problem of accomplishing long-term goals therefore is not the product of amateurs in government, or ideological rejection of planning, or even of "too much" participation.[27] Rather, it derives from inadequate continuity in political instruction and oversight.

Even when components of a ministry in France are moved, something that happens with less frequency than in Britain, the unit remains intact and the mandate remains immutable. Each unit retains certain sovereign powers, which are enhanced by ministerial turnover. Unable to assert much control or direction, French ministers rely on expert civil servants to make policy. Bureaucratic domains are insulated from the shocks of politics, a practice that guarantees policy continuity despite political turmoil. English-speaking people have borrowed both the term and the concept of *étatisme* from the French with good reason.

Political instability thus leads to different outcomes because it is part of different political systems. In one system it yields continuity, whereas in the other it yields discontinuity. Nevertheless, in certain circumstances it may produce common outcomes because the common characteristics of the political systems may dominate. British and French political systems are both parliamentary. Governments in both countries are able to pass legislation often scrutinized and understood by only a handful of elected Cabinet ministers. Given a similar willingness to manage news, manipulate choice, and deceive concerned citizens, both countries were able to approve the expenditures proposed for Concorde by private manufacturing interests, engineers, and technocrats. The automatic majority is a far more potent weapon than the vote of confidence, and the ability of narrow interests to capture both the public imagination and the machinery of government, in the end, may be an indictment of parliamentary democracy.

Policy uncertainty and Anglo-French uniqueness

Permanent infrastructure, not needed when built, occasionally does rescue the reputation of designers over time. Airport overconstruction at various sites in the United States, such as Dallas–Fort Worth and Atlanta, appeared justified in the 1980s with the reorientation of transfer traffic. Overconstruction at Edmonton, Alberta, became justified with the Canadian west's oil boom. It is easy to argue that in some distant future Paris will surely escape the traffic congestion that inevitably will befall London. Negative traffic forecasts will not necessarily prove more reliable than bad positive ones. The white elephants may eventually age gray and surrender great tusks of irony.

The British and French thus are hardly unique in their choice of projects, their developmental optimism, or their record of accomplishment. The TriStar L1011 that broke Rolls Royce also broke Lockheed, and production of the plane subsequently was abandoned after a rash of engine failures. As the British had to bail out Rolls Royce, so the Americans bailed out Lockheed, and Chrysler too. Dulles International Airport, the federal facility in Washington, D.C., is no less a white elephant than Charles de Gaulle Airport in Paris.

Britain and France may be no worse than other industrialized countries managing expensive new technology

(Tokyo's Narita Airport and West Germany's fast-breeder reactor program are two salient examples), but they are not apparently better. Neither affords the industrial world a model to emulate, despite the abundant literature supporting certain myths, especially about France. This point is important particularly because of the vigorous French campaign to claim such superiority in promoting products and consulting services in the Third World.

Origins of different institutions

Despite this emphasis on the similarity of failure and the examples that abound throughout the advanced industrial world, British and French institutions are different enough to produce different outcomes in the solving of common problems. It could be argued that such institutional differences are a reflection of different cultures and values and that the distinction between cultural and institutional causes therefore is artificial.

Institutions evolve as responses to historical circumstance and undoubtedly are nurtured by prevailing values. However, if in these cases the institutions were stripped away and only collections of French and British officials remained, one could not expect the outcomes that in fact were produced. The French and British officials of the postwar world, free of their institutions, likely would produce the same solutions to common problems because they so fundamentally share values and goals. Moreover, French officials governing British institutions probably could not have produced "French" solutions. Cultural transformation, implicated in so much social science about Western Europe, could not change the policies that were processed by distinct institutions. Individuals, and organizations of individuals, may commit the same errors or divine the same solutions, but they necessarily remain somewhat captive within their institutions.

Institutions order participation. They permit some voices to be heard while denying access to others. Dissenters over airport development and over Concorde were present in both Britain and France. In Britain they were heard; in France they were not. Doubters were present among the civil servants, and among the politicians, in both countries. No Briton questioned Concorde more vigorously than Jean-Jacques Servan-Schreiber. Although one might argue that Britain values dissent more than France, and that institutions are organized accordingly, in the presence of like personalities one set of institutions organizes the political process differently from another. Institutional origin thus is a challenging historical question, but it does not endow culture with much explanatory power for contrasts in public policy.

Beyond Britain and France

The problems that beset Britain and France in their competition with the United States, and with each other, may be symptomatic of a broader condition. Talk in the early 1980s of a general European malaise appeared as a renewal of perceived inferiority to U.S. industrial and entrepreneurial skill. There were expressions of familiar feelings about a European inability to get things done, manifested in unabated rates of unemployment and industrial stagnation. Incumbent governments relying on state authority for economic improvement faced extreme unpopularity or electoral failure.

The Concorde experience, in particular, may provide some clues to the perceptions that seem to dominate the malaise. Experts have come to dominate bureaucracies. Politicians have been either unwilling or unable to govern, whether because of inherent systemic weakness or because of susceptibility to the perceived requisites of democracy. Policies that may serve only narrow interests therefore may survive, precisely because specialists and experts are not expected to bear in mind the public interest yet are entrusted increasingly with authority.

Specialists and experts are trained to focus on narrow mandates and maximize their own objectives. They are not particularly skilled at negotiation and compromise. Technicians often agree, but above all when they perceive the problems they are confronting as apolitical. Top-level political consultation occurred frequently during the development of Concorde precisely because technical solutions invariably were political in character and technicians from different political systems therefore could not agree.

Within most of the European countries, and even among members of the European communities, a growing number of technical disputes are coming to the attention of senior elected officials for resolution. Some bemoan political interference while others applaud the emergence of popular sovereignty, but until politicians seize control of their own political systems by reducing discontinuity in decision making (the British problem) or bureaucratic insulation from politics (the French problem), they cannot expect their civil servants to reach the international negotiating table to resolve disputes without political intervention. The ministerial agenda will necessarily become crowded more and more by an accumulation of technical problems because of the authority of expertise.

The aircraft industry and the unions encouraged Concorde because the state guaranteed their incomes. This problem plagues all state enterprise and all private enterprise protected by the state. It is an important part of Europe's problem maintaining a Common Agricultural Policy, just as it has been a problem of restoring an aircraft industry. There is no simple formula for weaning industry from the state's teat, but surely it is time to challenge some doctrinal sacred cows, be they French central planning or the alleged calamity of British public participation.

One place to begin this challenge is with a recognition

that more open political processes do not assure failure and that the enforcement of political will over bureaucratic preference does not constitute interference with technical processes. Governments in parliamentary systems might choose their ministers with a greater sensitivity for the politician's own expertise and interest. More knowledgeable and interested ministers might, in turn, stay longer on their jobs, not to become political advocates for the narrow expertise they employ but rather to assimilate expert advice into the competitive mix of politics.

There is always a danger that a minister may remain at a post too long or become the political instrument of narrow interests. There is no simple solution to this risk, but the inherent tendency of parliamentary democracy appears to encourage nothing of the kind. Therefore, a conscientious effort to generate greater continuity and stability might merely offset on the margin the natural flow of political change. Such an adjustment, however modest, might return politics to public choice and improve the prospects for more satisfying outcomes. Although the policy process could be slowed by such a change, the legitimacy of political systems depends upon a kind of popular support not typically summoned by the technocrat.

In the arena of public works, decision making has broad economic consequence that is underappreciated. Prestige is imagined a worthy substitute for practicality, and technocratic dreams may be fulfilled through the honor apparently bestowed upon politicians. Monuments may make proud the élites who erect them, but history ridicules white elephants, and nobody loves an albatross. Concorde, however spelled, may in the end contribute less to Anglo-French friendship than to more effective dissent.

Epilogue

Although enough time has passed to enable political analysis of these cases, the stories have not yet ended. The update that follows inevitably will be dated again by the time of publication, but it may be useful to recognize the continuing direction of governmental choice.

Concorde flies to Miami, although the U.S. capital has been abandoned. The president of the French Republic has chartered the plane, as have British tourists on day trips to the Nile. Although Concorde is little more than a novelty, in 1985 there are still a few in the air.

The Government of Margaret Thatcher is privatizing British Airways, a step that may accelerate the termination of Concorde services: Shareholders scrutinizing the balance sheets may be impressed by the revenues of the London–New York route, but they are unlikely to show much enthusiasm for the overall economic impact of Concorde on BA's fleet.

Gatwick has a satellite terminal, linked to the main terminal by a short and efficient rail line, and the opening of Heathrow's fourth terminal is imminent. Shortly after coming to power, the Thatcher Government declared an interest in the development of Stansted to meet air traffic needs in southeast England. A 258-day public inquiry followed in 1984, and in December the inquiry inspector dutifully recommended the immediate expansion of Stansted into London's third international airport. The report ridicules previous governments for vacillation (a rather blatant appeal to Mrs. Thatcher's self-image), particularly for failing to build a second runway at Gatwick and a fifth terminal at Heathrow. Although the first option is foreclosed, the second is advocated: The report recommends immediate clearance of the sewage works as part of a package of improvements to accommodate traffic, projected to grow from 43 million passengers in 1984 to 93 million in the next decade. The forecast is yet another extrapolation doubling traffic at ten-year intervals, this time without additional runways.

The report's publication stimulated not a word of endorsement from the media, and the London *Times*'s lead read, "MPs of all parties last night braced themselves to oppose the recommendations." A Commons motion included the signatures of ninety-five members of Mrs. Thatcher's party. The most significant new feature of the debate is Britain's sweeping unemployment. In 1984 Stansted is opposed above all because MPs from all parts of the country think the £1 billion or more to be invested should reach the hardest-hit regions rather than help sustain the southeast. The environment is a secondary issue, and the economics of airport questions and traffic demand is exclusively a concern of the Government and the British Airports Authority.

Two of the three parts of Charles de Gaulle's Terminal 2 are open, and Roissy Rail is tied into the Paris regional transport system. It is now possible to board in the center of Paris and go directly to the airport without changing trains at Gare du Nord. Although considerable traffic has been generated along the route, the airport remains the destination of few passengers availing themselves of the more efficient system. And French television has featured stories about the plight of villages subjected to the noise of the Paris airports.

Methodological appendix: Comparative politics and case studies

This book may provoke questions about the utility of both comparative and case studies. Because the case method depends on detail, there is a tendency to see each case or experience as unique. Can case studies be the basis for generalizations? Can they be used to formulate theory? And because comparisons often are derived from the details of more than one example, experience, or country, there is a need to establish that the items (examples, experiences, or even countries) are genuinely comparable. Curiously, although comparisons imply the use of cases, the two traditions rarely have been combined.

THE UTILITY OF CASE STUDIES

There can be no doubt that the case study has always been a rich source of primary data that can direct attention to neglected aspects of the political process.[1] The essential criticisms of the method have been of the arbitrary selection of data and of the accidental, unsystematic way comparisons are drawn.

Harry Eckstein claims that a single "crucial" case can be a rigorous and decisive form of hypothesis testing.[2] The task, he says, is to "fit" the case to existing theory. Arend Lijphart has called such cases "theory-confirming" and "theory-infirming," and they support the proposition that if one case can contribute to theory, more than one, carefully selected and defined, can be even more useful.[3] Moreover, according to Alexander George, the number of cases "need not be representative in the statistical sampling sense in order to contribute to theory development. The desideratum that guides selection of cases in the controlled comparison approach is not numbers but *variety*, that is, cases belonging to the same class that differ from each other. Thus, the investigator in designing the study will either seek cases in which the outcome of the dependent variable differed or cases having the same outcome but a different explanation for it."[4] One case, by these arguments, may contribute to theory, however debatable may be the "crucial" character of the selected case; two cases, accordingly, may be sufficient for theory building in comparative politics.

COMPARISON WITHOUT CASES

The study of comparative politics has been pursued with many methods. According to Robert Golembiewski, William Welsh, and William Crotty, "In the twentieth century approaches to comparative politics may be summarized in three categories: 'philosophic traditionalists,' 'model-builders,' and 'mathematizers-quantifiers.' "[5] Notable for its conspicuous absence from this list is the case study, accused by these same authors of being "much ado about virtually nothing."[6] Roy Macridis and Bernard Brown complained in the 1950s that cases were done singly as descriptive monographs that did not contribute to theory,[7] and according to Alexander George by the end of the 1960s the case study had fallen into disrepute.[8] Not only was it absent from the respected methods of comparative politics; it was rejected throughout political science.

The bad reputation of case studies through the 1960s can be attributed to their configurative and isolated character, to the failure to select cases in different settings for their common attributes. No serious comparison was in fact undertaken, so there could be no test of the utility of the method. Area studies undermined comparative analysis by encouraging single-country inquiries, and when several political systems were studied with the same theoretical framework, there was still no deliberate cross-national comparison of experience.[9]

Survey research was perceived by many scholars as an ideal method for making cross-national comparisons. The comparison of cases generally was not tried, and one might suppose that scholars feared the difficulties associated with the identification of cases sufficiently common in their attributes, because the many details inevitably would be peculiar to each particular case. Surveys, however, were easy to control: The scholar needed only to ask the same question of respondents in different places.

The absence of case studies in comparative politics seems to reflect less on the case study itself than on the problem of equivalence. This problem, however, is posed for all comparative methods, and the case study indeed often may be a better solution than many other methods available.

THE PROBLEM OF EQUIVALENCE

One can never be sure that a problem in one place is the same as a problem in another. Even when the technical features of a problem appear identical, actors in one place may give these features different priorities or significance than the actors in a second place. The scholar who frames a common question has no guarantee that it will be understood in the same way in more than one place. Language is of course one source of misunderstanding, but there are many other filters for meaning, including race, class, or political position. Perspective may redefine a question as much as language.

For these reasons, surveys can be no more reliable in overcoming the problem of equivalence than other available methods. Indeed, anthropologists and sociologists often have doubted whether any comparison can be accomplished usefully. Terence Tatje complains that "in comparative research different operational measures of the 'same' theoretical concept are often employed,"[10] and in a survey of empirical studies in anthropology Robert Hunt concludes variously that "one looks in vain for measures," or "no confidence can be placed in the results."[11] His references are to the absence of systematic controls for equivalence. R. Bruce Anderson has queried, "How do we know we are asking the same question in two or more settings,"[12] and Rodney Needham has concluded that comparison itself is impossible, so dominated is it by the futile search for equivalence.[13]

However futile the search, comparison is a permanent feature of social science, because, as Hunt suggests, "Comparison is the only means we have of acquiring knowledge."[14] No object of study can have significance unless it is measured against some other object or standard, and significance is necessarily a measure of something's being more important than something else. Even if perfect equivalence can never be achieved, all social scientists strive for an approximation, and students of comparative politics bear a particular responsibility for struggling with this problem systematically.

Once the case method is accepted as a useful tool for the formulation and development of theory, it is appropriate to consider how it may be deployed effectively in comparative studies. There are at least two schools of thought. One, exemplified by Adam Przeworski and Henry Teune, recommends the study of "most different cases."[15] The other, defended by Lijphart, says that when similarities dominate, differences are easier to explain, and that the object of the exercise is to explain differences.[16] Unfortunately, as Robert K. Yin points out, "The case-comparison approach [has not] been sufficiently documented to produce a specific set of guidelines for future research."[17] It is thus possible to argue for the comparison of highly similar or highly contrasting cases.

Despite this disagreement among scholars, the stronger arguments seem to have accrued progressively around the position taken by Lijphart. Alexander George recommends, above all, the "controlled comparison," and he has explained why the case study has been so little used for comparisons in the past: "One reason why single case studies in the past contributed so little to theory development was that they either lacked a common focus or a common approach to the study of a given type of problem."[18] George's "method of structured, focused comparison" is an elaboration of Lijphart's "comparable cases," decidedly a preference for explaining differences through "most similar" experiences.[19]

Sidney Verba has supported the use of case studies in comparative analysis by arguing that cases identify patterns discernible in the cases under study and in still other cases.[20] The Canadian-American comparisons of Christopher Leman, Seymour Martin Lipset, and Robert Presthus sustain this view and add weight to the most-similar-systems approach.[21] It is clear from this literature that rigorous case selection across countries can maximize similarities and enable intelligent explanation of differences.

The utility of such explanatory power lies in the potential for theory development. Employing Harry Eckstein's "crucial" and "heuristic" case approach (but criticizing Eckstein for failure to recognize the application of *comparison* to single case studies), Alexander George concludes: "Actually, a *series* of heuristic case studies or a simultaneous comparison of two or more cases, if each comprises an instance of the same class of events, can be an excellent research strategy for the cumulative development of theory."[22] Hence well-chosen cases may contribute to theory, and systematically selected cases that highlight different outcomes to highly similar problems within similar systems can move comparative analysis toward its greatest theoretical promise.

Regrettably, one can never be certain that a chosen case indeed is crucial or heuristic. There can be no certainty that a particular case is representative of a country or a political system, or even of a category of cases. The rich detail of case studies opens them to charges of peculiarity, whereas aggregate studies, usually omitting contextual detail, are less vulnerable to this criticism. However, aggregate studies are far more vulnerable to the claim that they are unrealistic and do not appreciate the context or subtlety of the systems or countries they analyze. They may be representative only at a level of generalization or abstraction that provides little or no guidance for actual, specific experience. They may yield theories that seem to explain everything in general but nothing in particular.

Cases may never be "equivalent," but they may reveal sufficiently similar patterns, or bear sufficiently similar characteristics, to justify systematic comparisons and contrasts. There may be enough points in common to facilitate explanation of the causes of difference, and those causes may refer to general conditions or characteristics of the respective systems. As Robert Hunt has concluded, "The controlled comparison is the most effective in solving for equivalence. In this strategy one attempts the smallest possible sample size, and to match the systems of interest on all variables but those which are part of the hypothesis."[23]

TWO WHITE ELEPHANTS AND ONE ALBATROSS

The cases in this book were chosen according to Lijphart's criteria as "hypothesis-generating" or "deviant,"[24] and they were used as Joseph LaPalombara recommends, for the formulation of middle-range propositions concerning partial systems.[25] Comparison was used in Hugh Stretton's sense, not as an experiment leading to simple answers but as a stimulus to the imagination and a generator of new questions.[26]

It is difficult in all instances to be sure whether the systems in which these cases are set conform to a most-similar or most-different approach. Commonly the latter would seem to refer to systems highly contrasting in industrial development or geographical distance or population disparity. A comparison of an African with a European country would seem more obviously consistent with the most-different-systems approach than the comparison pursued here between Britain and France. Yet, as emphasized in Chapter 1, Britain and France traditionally have been a starting point for students contrasting political systems and cultures. Because an argument of this book is that the systems are more similar than commonly supposed, the hypothesis to be tested necessarily has conformed to the most-different approach. The white elephants constitute cases in which technical variables are constant and, on examination, official attitudes and perceptions also are constant. Hence the cases are highly similar, within hypothetically different political systems. The task has been to explain the different outcomes of the case experiences.

One obvious avenue to explanation, which would have confirmed the hypothesis, would have emphasized cultural differences. This explanation failed. However, institutional differences did prove highly explanatory. As the cultures were similar, the systems were indeed significantly different. The cases were sufficiently similar to enable reaching such a conclusion reliably.

One may object that despite the consistency of technical variables, and even of official definitions and priorities, the airport problem in Britain and France was not precisely the same. The French had land to spare and the British had none; the French assessed a new airport as an opportunity while the British thought of one as a necessity. The British calculated their needs as an island, whereas the French looked upon their requirements as a Continental country with complementary transportation systems. Although it has been possible to answer such doubts on their merits, the inclusion of Concorde among the case studies has provided a more definitive response.

Whereas issues of airport development were decided independently in Britain and France (although at the same time), issues of a supersonic transport were decided jointly. The British and French assumed joint responsibility, shared expenses equally, and calculated the future collectively. Although Concorde promised different advantages for each, the task of construction and marketing, as a joint venture, was necessarily the same. The two systems had to deal simultaneously with the same problem. The outcome, of course, could not be different because it was a joint venture, but the sources of difficulty indeed could be different, and they highlighted the points of similarity and difference in the policy-making apparatus of the two countries.

No two cases, in the end, are precisely the same. Differences, however, vary in importance depending on how carefully the cases have been chosen. Although "care" is subject only to a relative measure, control of the technical variables in high technology and the cultural variables among decision-making élites does afford reliable comparisons of public choice. Other controls may be appropriate for other cases in which the same general rule applies: Comparability depends on discovering variation through the systematic control of common characteristics.

Notes

PREFACE
1   Harry Eckstein, "Case Study and Theory in Political Science," in
Fred Greenstein and Nelson Polsby, eds., *Handbook of Political Science*
(Reading, Mass.: Addison-Wesley, 1975), VII, p. 138.

CHAPTER 1. COMPARE OR CONTRAST?
1   The classic statement of the contrast is Edmund Burke, *Reflections
on the Revolution in France* (New York: Bobbs-Merrill for the Liberal Arts
Press, 1955).
2   Jack Hayward, "Institutional Inertia and Political Impetus in France
and Britain," *European Journal of Political Research* 4 (1976), pp. 341–59.
3   Andrew Shonfield, *Modern Capitalism: The Changing Balance of Public
and Private Power* (Oxford: Oxford University Press, 1965); Arnold J.
Heidenheimer, Hugh Heclo, and Carolyn Teich Adams, *Comparative
Public Policy: The Politics of Social Choice in Europe and America* (New York:
St. Martin's Press, 1975). See also Jean-Jacques Bonnaud, "Planning
and Industry in France," in Jack Hayward and Michael Watson, eds.,
*Planning, Politics and Public Policy: The British, French and Italian Experi-
ence* (Cambridge: Cambridge University Press, 1975), pp. 93–110, as an
example. There have been important French exceptions, especially Michel
Crozier's *The Bureaucratic Phenomenon* (Chicago: University of Chicago
Press, 1964) and *La société bloquée* (Paris: Seuil, 1970), as well as Pierre
Gremion's "La théorie de l'apprentissage institutionel," in Michel Crozier, ed., *Où va l'administration française?* (Paris: Editions Organisations,
1974). These statements are not representative, however, of most French
scholarship and opinion.
4   Peter A. Hall, "French Etatism versus British Pluralism," manuscript, Harvard University Center for European Studies, July 1978.
5   Samuel Beer, Suzanne Berger, Guido Goldman, and Adam Ulam,
Patterns of Government: The Major Political Systems of Europe (New York:
Random House, 1973).

6   Shonfield, *Modern Capitalism;* Jack Hayward, "Change and Choice: The Agenda of Planning," in Hayward and Watson, *Planning, Politics and Public Policy,* p. 6; Stephen Cohen, *Modern Capitalist Planning: The French Model* (Cambridge, Mass.: Harvard University Press, 1969); Vera Lutz, *Central Planning for the Market Economy: An Analysis of the French Theory and Experience* (London: Longmans, 1969).

7   Shonfield, *Modern Capitalism,* especially chap. 5.

8   See Robert Gilpin, *France in the Age of the Scientific State* (Princeton, N.J.: Princeton University Press, 1968).

9   Suzanne Berger, in Beer et al., *Patterns of Government,* p. 420. This view is representative of a substantial literature, both from early work (e.g., Mark Kesselman, *The Ambiguous Consensus: A Study of Local Government in France* [New York: Knopf, 1967]) and from more recent repetitions of an apparent article of faith (e.g., William Safran, *The French Polity* [New York: McKay, 1977], especially pp. 231–4).

10   Shonfield, *Modern Capitalism,* pp. 144–5, 171.

11   The first notable critique was developed empirically by Jerome Milch; see his "Paris Is Not France: Policy Outputs and Political Values in Two French Cities," doctoral diss., MIT, 1973. Since that study other contributions include Howard Machin, "Local Government Change in France – The Case of the 1964 Reforms," *Policy and Politics* 3, no. 2 (1974); Douglas Ashford, "Are Britain and France 'Unitary'?" *Comparative Politics* 9 (July 1977), pp. 483–99; and Douglas Ashford, *English Centralism and French Pragmatism: Central–Local Policymaking in the Welfare State* (London: Allen & Unwin, 1982).

12   Henry Ehrmann, "Politics in France," in Gabriel Almond and G. Bingham Powell, Jr., eds., *Comparative Politics Today: A World View,* 2d ed. (Boston: Little, Brown, 1980); Barbara N. McLennan, *Comparative Politics and Public Policy* (North Scituate, Mass.: Duxbury Press, 1980), chaps. 6 and 13. These books are recent examples.

13   Robert A. Isaak, *European Politics: Political Economy and Policy Making in Western Democracies* (New York: St. Martin's Press, 1980); Charles F. Andrain, *Politics and Economic Policy in Western Democracies* (North Scituate, Mass.: Duxbury Press, 1980). These recent examples also reflect the influence of academic fads; although the titles carry the key words "policy" and "political economy," the analytical assumptions about the influence of particular institutions and interests remain entirely conventional and dependent upon a secondary literature.

14   Berger, in Beer et al., *Patterns of Government,* p. 424; Ezra Suleiman, *Politics, Power and Bureaucracy in France: The Administrative Elite* (Princeton, N.J.: Princeton University Press, 1974); Jean-Claude Thoenig, *L'ere des technocrates* (Paris: Editions Organisations, 1973); Vincent Wright, *Government and Politics of France,* 2d ed., rev. (London: Hutchinson, 1983).

15   Cohen, *Modern Capitalist Planning,* p. 153.

16   Ibid., p. 154; see also Hayward and Watson, *Planning, Politics, and Public Policy.*
17   John McArthur and Bruce Scott, *Industrial Planning in France* (Boston: Harvard Business School, 1969), p. 501.
18   Hall, "French Etatism."
19   Samuel Beer, *British Politics in the Collectivist Age* (New York: Random House, Vintage Books, 1965), chap. 12; Jack Hayward, "Institutional Inertia," in Hayward and Watson, *Planning, Politics and Public Policy.*
20   Shonfield, *Modern Capitalism*, pp. 88, 112, 110.
21   For the most thorough critique of pluralism, see Theodore J. Lowi, *The End of Liberalism* (New York: Norton, 1969).
22   The argument was made powerfully first by Grant McConnell, *Private Power and American Democracy* (New York: Knopf, 1966).
23   Jack Hayward, "The Politics of Planning in France and Britain," *Comparative Politics*, January 1975, p. 288.
24   Most recently, S. E. Finer, *The Changing British Party System, 1945– 1979* (Washington, D.C.: American Enterprise Institute, 1980).
25   David Butler and Donald Stokes, *Political Change in Britain: The Evolution of Electoral Choice*, 2d ed. (New York: St. Martin's Press, 1974).
26   Bruce E. Cain, "Challenges and Responses in British Party Politics," *Comparative Politics*, April 1980; Ivor Crewe, Bo Sarlvik, and James Alt, "Partisan Dealignment in Britain, 1964–1974," *British Journal of Political Science*, April 1977; Bo Sarlvik and Ivor Crewe, *The Conservative Victory of 1979* (Cambridge: Cambridge University Press, 1983).
27   Finer, *Changing British Party System.*
28   Shonfield, *Modern Capitalism*, pp. 156–8; this theme can be found throughout Hayward's work.
29   Jack Hayward, "National Aptitudes for Planning in Britain, France and Italy," *Government and Opposition*, Autumn 1974, p. 407.
30   Beer, in Beer et al., *Patterns of Government*, p. 170.
31   Jack Hayward, "Have British Planners Learnt from Experience?" *Government and Opposition*, Winter 1979, p. 122.
32   Ibid., pp. 121–2.
33   An important example of a single case in a single country presenting these views is John Zysman's study of the French electronics industry in *Political Strategies for Industrial Order* (Berkeley: University of California Press, 1977).
34   Discussion may be found in Elliot J. Feldman, "Comparative Public Policy: Field or Method?" *Comparative Politics*, Winter 1978, pp. 287– 305, with particular reference to Heidenheimer, Heclo, and Adams, *Comparative Public Policy*, and Hayward and Watson, *Planning, Politics and Public Policy.*
35   For a quaint and pessimistic picture of the situation and the fu-

ture, see B. J. Hurren, *Britain and World Air Transport* (London: John Crowther, 1943).

CHAPTER 2. THE PARISIAN WHITE ELEPHANT

1   Pierre Donatien Cot, addressing the Cercle Culturel de Royaumont, June 1963, quoted by Gilbert Dreyfus, "Il fallait construire l'aéroport de Roissy-en-France," in *Roissy en France* (Paris: Aéroport de Paris, 1973). This point was also emphasized by the responsible minister of the period, Marc Jacquet, in an interview in Paris, June 9, 1975.

2   See Robert Gilpin, *France in the Age of the Scientific State* (Princeton, N.J.: Princeton University Press, 1968), especially p. 339, on the linkage of technical achievement to French perceptions of international status. François de Closets, in *La France et ses mensonges* (Paris: Denoël/Gonthier, 1978), argues that criticism of civil aviation, the "cherished daughter of Gaullist Science," was the ultimate taboo in France; see especially pp. 22–4.

3   Numerous documents published by Aéroport de Paris, beginning in 1967, reiterate the offical explanations. Particularly revealing and detailed examples are in *Roissy en France;* see especially the articles by Dreyfus, Aéroport de Paris director general ("Il fallait constuire l'aéroport de Roissy-en-France"), and Jacques Block, deputy director general ("L'aéroport de Roissy-en-France et son environment").

4   A revealing report may be found in the cover story of *Aéroports Magazine*, no. 61, April 1976, published by Aéroport de Paris.

5   Expropriation was the trigger to airport development conflicts in Frankfurt, Milan, Vancouver, and Tokyo, and the threat of it incited protest in New York, Toronto, and London.

6   Interview with Marc Jacquet, Paris, June 9, 1975.

7   Interview with Louis Lesieux, Paris, October 18, 1976.

8   Kenneth R. Sealy, *Airport Strategy and Planning* (Oxford: Oxford University Press, 1976); Richard de Neufville, *Airport Systems Planning* (Cambridge, Mass.: MIT Press, 1976).

9   For a discussion of the "environmental airport," see Elliot J. Feldman and Jerome Milch, "Options on the Metropolitan Fringe: Strategies of Airport Development," in Douglas Ashford, ed., *National Resources and Urban Policy* (New York: Methuen, 1980), pp. 215–38.

10   The required separating distance for the simultaneous use of parallel runways is disputed and depends upon navigational aids at least as much as upon air turbulence. Furthermore, instances of such simultaneous use are rare in even the busiest airports. Officials at the International Civil Aviation Organization, which sets guidelines for air safety, reckon the safe distance as somewhere between four thousand and five thousand feet, but Aéroport de Paris officials insisted on a minimum of

one mile in the name of technical expertise and safety. Interview with Kenneth Wilde, ICAO Airport Service, Montreal, October 7, 1976.

11 Prevailing winds mattered a good deal when commercial aircraft were light; despite the greater operational independence of heavier planes, airport planners still prefer to follow prevailing winds. Most runways throughout Europe, therefore, are built east–west.

12 French forecasts, like forecasts elsewhere, have declined in accuracy over time despite improvements and greater sophistication in technique. The main, consistent weakness derives from reliance on extrapolation. For discussion of this forecasting pattern, see Elliot J. Feldman and Jerome Milch, *Technocracy versus Democracy: The Comparative Politics of International Airports* (Boston: Auburn House, 1982), chap. 3.

13 Decret No. 47-11 du 4 Janvier 1947.

14 See especially Commissariat Général du Plan, *Rapport de la Commission des Transports et Communications, Préparation du 7e Plan* (Paris: La Documentation Française, 1976).

15 Organisme Régional d'Etudes Pour l'Aménagement de la Picardie, *Le Sud de la Picardie et l'Aéroport Charles de Gaulle* (Amiens: OREAP, 1974).

16 Various press reports were confirmed in interviews with Antoine Veil, president of UTA, Puteaux, December 17, 1976, and René Lapautre, director general of Air Inter, Paris, October 22, 1976.

17 This experience is similar to that of Montreal, where, after the inauguration of Mirabel, passengers rerouted through Toronto to avoid Mirabel–Dorval transfers. In the Canadian context such overflying drew passenger traffic away from a particular airport but not the flag carrier; in the European setting the consequence can be loss of traffic to another country's airline. See Elliot J. Feldman and Jerome Milch, *The Politics of Canadian Airport Development: Lessons for Federalism* (Durham, N.C.: Duke University Press, 1983).

18 Interview with Veil, Puteaux, December 17, 1976.

19 See, for example, the statement by F. Ailleret, "L'exploitation des aérogares, passagers, et de fret à Roissy," in *Roissy en France*, p. 35.

20 This view was expressed both by George Vincer Hole (former undersecretary in the Ministry of Aviation and former chief executive of the British Airports Authority and president of the Western European Airports Association), in an interview in London, January 4, 1977, and by Norman Payne, former director of the British Airports Authority, in an interview in London, January 12, 1977.

21 On the weakness and reality of the *tutelle*, see Pierre Gremion, "La théorie de l'apprentissage institutionel," in Michel Crozier, ed., *Où va l'administration française?* (Paris: Editions Organisations, 1974). Oversight for Aéroport de Paris comes from a staff of fewer than five people.

CHAPTER 3. THE IMPERIAL WHITE ELEPHANT HUNT

1   Peter Hall, in *Great Planning Disasters* (Berkeley: University of California Press, 1980), has tried to compare the planning of the third London Airport with that for other projects that were actually executed, but the analysis is troublesome.

2   In addition to many articles, there are several books: Olive Cook, *The Stansted Affair: A Case for the People* (London: Pan Books, 1967); David Perman, *Cublington: A Blueprint for Resistance* (London: Bodley Head, 1973); David McKie, *A Sadly Mismanaged Affair: A Political History of the Third London Airport* (London: Croom Helm, 1973); Peter Bromhead, *The Great White Elephant of Maplin Sands* (London: Paul Eletz, 1973).

3   This analysis applies especially to Roskill and Maplin; see, for example, Peter Self, "Cost–Benefit Analysis and the Roskill Commission," *Political Quarterly* 41, no. 3 (1970); E. J. Mishan, "What Is Wrong with Roskill?" *Journal of Transport Economics and Policy*, September 1970; and Christopher Foster, J. B. Heath, G. H. Peters, J. E. Ffowcs Williams, and Sir Peter Masefield, *Lessons of Maplin: Is the Machinery for Governmental Decision-Making at Fault?* (London: Institute of Economic Affairs, 1974).

4   Cook, *The Stansted Affair*; Perman, *Cublington*; Robert J. Scott, "The Jetport Location Dilemma: Politics, Parochialism, and the Public Interest," master's thesis, Cornell University, 1973.

5   British Airports Authority, *Report and Accounts 1966–67,* House of Commons Paper No. 583, 1966–7, pp. 11, 12.

6   This observation is based on confidential interviews with civil servants in several British agencies.

7   According to Susan Crosland, *Tony Crosland* (London: Jonathan Cape, 1982), the environmental super-ministry was planned by Labour in early 1970 (p. 264). Some movement of responsibilities does seem related to the strength and prestige of the minister, regardless of party.

8   *Report of the London Airport Development Committee,* CAP 145 (London: HMSO, 1957).

9   *Fifth Report from the Estimates Committee: London's Airports* (Session 1960–1, HCP 233) (London: HMSO), paras. 116, 142.

10   Ministry of Aviation, *Report of the Inter-Departmental Committee on the Third London Airport,* CAP 199 (London: HMSO, 1964).

11   Interview with George Hole, former undersecretary of the Ministry of Aviation and former chief executive of the BAA, in London, January 4, 1977.

12   Ministry of Housing and Local Government, *Report of the Inquiry into Local Objections to the Proposed Development of Land at Stansted as the Third London Airport* (London: HMSO, 1967).

13   Cmnd. 3259, *The Third London Airport* (London: HMSO, 1967).

Douglas Jay, who presented the white paper to Parliament, could not later remember that it called for four runways and indicated that he believed such a proposal probably unjustified. Interview with Douglas Jay, MP, in London, January 11, 1977.

14 The committee, chaired by George Hole, was composed of seven members from the Ministry of Aviation, four representatives from the airlines, one member from the Air Ministry (for defense purposes), two from Air Traffic Services, one from the Ministry of Transport (access), and one from Housing and Local Government.

15 Interview with Lord Boston, London, January 19, 1977.

16 A partial discussion noting the simultaneity of issues in Lords may be found in R. H. S. Crossman, *The Diaries of a Cabinet Minister, vol. II* (London: Hamish Hamilton & Jonathan Cape, 1968), p. 684. Lord Boston links the two issues more explicitly (ibid.), as does David McKie, "Buried in the Sands," *Guardian*, March 13, 1974.

17 Airports Authority Act, Elizabeth II, 1965, c. 16; the authority later added Edinburgh Airport, Aberdeen, and Glasgow.

18 Airports Authority Act, c. 1 (4).

19 British Airports Authority, *Report and Accounts 1968–69*, House of Commons Paper No. 377, 1968–9, p. 74.

20 Ibid., p. 73.

21 *Hansard's*, vol. 765, (May 20, 1968) col. 38.

22 Commission on the Third London Airport, *Report*, (London: HMSO, 1971).

23 Interview with Tony Flowerdew, deputy director of research for the Roskill Commission, London, January 6, 1977.

24 Commission on the Third London Airport, "Note of Dissent by Colin Buchanan," in Commission on the Third London Airport, *Report*, pp. 149–60. Buchanan apparently raised none of his objections during the deliberations of the commission.

25 Interview with John Davies, London, January 20, 1977.

26 Some interview respondents have denied that there was any CPRS review of Roskill.

27 It is often suggested that the Port of London Authority, involved with very substantial financial and construction interests, applied the principal pressure for adoption of the coastal site.

28 *Maplin: Review of Airport Project* (London: HMSO, 1974), pp. 41, 58.

29 Here and throughout "billion" signifies U.S. billion (thousand million).

30 Derrick Wood organized the opposition to construction at Foulness and Maplin Sands in defense of the natural environment. He persuaded the BBC to feature him often in television examinations of the subject; he gained access to Crosland, worked closely with Lord Boston,

and achieved greater notoriety and admiration than any other single figure opposing the third London airport at any site. Interview with Derrick Wood, Southend, January 17, 1977.
31   Cmnd. 7084, *Airports Policy* (London: HMSO, 1978).

CHAPTER 4. THE ALBATROSS

1   See, for example, Jean-Jacques Bonnaud, "Planning and Industry in France," in Jack Hayward and Michael Watson, eds., *Planning, Politics and Public Policy: The British, French and Italian Experience* (Cambridge: Cambridge University Press, 1975), pp. 93–110.
2   F. G. Clark and Arthur Gibson, *Concorde: The Story of the World's Most Advanced Passenger Aircraft* (London: Phoebus Publishing, 1976), p. 2.
3   Robert Gilpin, *France in the Age of the Scientific State* (Princeton, N.J.: Princeton University Press, 1968), p. 339.
4   Clark and Gibson, *Concorde*, p. 2.
5   John Costello and Terry Hughes, *Concorde Conspiracy* (New York: Scribner's, 1976).
6   John Davis, *The Concorde Affair* (London: Frewin, 1969).
7   Andrew Wilson, *The Concorde Fiasco* (Harmondsworth: Penguin Books, 1973), pp. 9–10.
8   Richard Wiggs, *Concorde: The Case Against Supersonic Transport* (London: Ballantine for Friends of the Earth, 1971), p. ix.
9   Peter Hall, *Great Planning Disasters* (Berkeley: University of California Press, 1980).
10   Jean Forestier, "Concorde: Le pari du vieux continent," *AviMag* 672 (December 15, 1975), pp. 36–43.
11   François de Closets, *La France et ses mensonges* (Paris: Editions Denöel/Gonthier, 1978), particularly chap. 2, "Concorde: L'oiseu du tabou."
12   Annabelle May, "Concorde – Bird of Harmony or Political Albatross: An Examination in the Context of British Foreign Policy," *International Organization* 33 (Autumn 1979), pp. 481–508.
13   Cmnd. 1916, *Agreement between the Government of the United Kingdom of Great Britain and Northern Ireland and the Government of the French Republic regarding the Development and Production of a Civil Supersonic Transport Aircraft* (London: HMSO, 1962).
14   Wilson, *The Concorde Fiasco*, p. 26.
15   See especially Costello and Hughes, *Concorde Conspiracy;* Wilson, *The Concorde Fiasco;* and May, "Concorde – Bird of Harmony."
16   Quoted in May, "Concorde – Bird of Harmony," p. 486.
17   See Richard E. Neustadt, *Alliance Politics* (New York: Columbia University Press, 1970).
18   Such a conclusion does not, however, implicate the FCO, whose

involvement was summoned by other departments, including Defence, Trade, and Industry, because the project involved a foreign country. The FCO did not initiate Concorde, or sign its treaty, or carry any subsequent negotiations. Interview with Stephen Barrett, former director for science and technology in the FCO, Boston, March 3, 1978.

19   Amery emphasized that during the negotiation the responsible French minister changed three times, shifts that left him the most constant participant; he also was helped by his relationship to the prime minister, who was his father-in-law. Interview with Julian Amery, London, June 13, 1978.

20   The role of the unions is discussed by Wilson in *The Concorde Fiasco*, pp. 39–46.

21   The Chambrun affair was exposed in *Le Canard Enchaîné* but ignored in the conventional press. François de Closets discusses the affair in *La France et ses mensonges*, pp. 51–4.

22   Anthony Wedgwood Benn to the House of Commons, March 19, 1974.

23   Emphasized by Davis, *The Concorde Affair.*

24   Clark and Gibson, *Concorde.*

25   Ibid.

26   Wilson, *The Concorde Fiasco*, pp. 72 ff.

27   Interview with Raymond Nivet, deputy director of technical development for Air France, Paris, May 30, 1978.

28   Milton S. Hochmuth, *Organizing the Transnational: The Experience with Transnational Enterprise in Advanced Technology* (Leiden: A. W. Sijthoff, 1974), pp. 126–56.

29   Confidential interview with senior civil servant, Ministry of Transport and Civil Aviation, Paris, May 29, 1978.

30   Owing to an industrywide recession, Airbus did not sell well before 1976 despite the delays. In this respect the impact of Concorde was fortuitous.

31   R. A. McCrindle and P. Godfrey, *Investigation into Rolls Royce* (London: HMSO, 1973).

32   Press conference, February 7, 1971.

33   *Aviation Week and Space Technology,* November 13, 1972.

34   Quoted in *Aviation Week and Space Technology,* August 23, 1976, p. 29; this view was confirmed in detail in an interview with Gordon Davidson, London, June 5, 1978.

35   David L. Nicolson to the Hon. Peter Shore, MP, April 9, 1974, in British Airways, "Concorde Appraisal" (Mimeographed, London, 1974).

36   Minister of transport to director of Air France, February 28, 1963.

37   On January 21, 1974, *Aviation Week and Space Technology* published confidential memorandums referring to August 1973 decisions.

38   Cited in *Aviation Week and Space Technology,* May 26, 1980.

39   Private correspondence with senior French civil servant in Ministry of Transport and Civil Aviation, March 1982.
40   Confidential interviews with aviation officials.
41   Confidential interview.
42   Quoted in *Fortune*, January 30, 1978, p. 67.
43   Such operations were to be the essence of Concorde's future, according to Clark and Gibson, *Concorde*, p. 64.

CHAPTER 5. POLITICAL INSTABILITY AND HIGH TECHNOLOGY

1   A typical example is Jean Forestier, "Concorde: Le pari du vieux continent," *AviMag* 672 (December 15, 1975), p. 39.
2   The best study probably is Robert Putnam, *The Beliefs of Politicians: Ideology, Conflict, and Democracy in Britain and Italy* (New Haven, Conn.: Yale University Press, 1973). Putnam acknowledges in detail the problem of linking attitudes to behavior, but his solution is a disappointing commitment to words as actions on the grounds that discourse is the behavior of politicians. See especially the discussion at pp. 25–7.
3   Olive Cook, *The Stansted Affair: A Case for the People* (London: Pan Books, 1967), p. 51.
4   This trait is considered by some an essential French weakness. An important exponent of this view is Alain Peyrefitte, *Le mal français* (Paris: Librairie Plon, 1976).
5   Anglo-American relations, even in conflicts such as Suez or Skybolt, have been conducted as a negotiating partnership among bureaucrats and political officials without recourse to the courts or Congress or Parliament. For discussion of the conduct of relations, see Richard E. Neustadt, *Alliance Politics* (New York: Columbia University Press, 1970).
6   David Henderson, "Two British Errors: Their Probable Size and Some Possible Lessons," *Oxford Economic Papers* 29 (July 1977); François de Closets, *La France et ses mensonges* (Paris: Denoël/Gonthier, 1978).
7   Confidential interview with *haut fonctionnaire* responsible for providing written answers to deputies of the National Assembly, Paris, May 1978.
8   Interview with Julian Amery, London, June 13, 1978.
9   Raymond Nivet, "An Airline's Approach to Aircraft Selection," speech delivered to the Royal Aeronautical Society, Dublin Branch, January 17, 1977, p. 4.
10   Quoted in *L'Humanité*, April 2, 1974.
11   Jack Hayward, "Have British Planners Learnt from Experience?" *Government and Opposition*, Winter 1979, pp. 121–2.
12   Andrew Shonfield, *Modern Capitalism: The Changing Balance of Public and Private Power* (Oxford: Oxford University Press, 1965), p. 226.

13   Pierre Massé, "L'Europe et l'idée de programmation économique," *Révue du Marché Commun*, no. 55, February 1963, p. 50.

14   Although in both Britain and France it was argued that the unions would not permit cancellation of Concorde, survey results did not agree. In a poll conducted by the *London Observer*, February 14, 1974, 50 percent of trade unionists recommended cancellation, compared to 34 percent who wanted continuation; the largest single group supporting continuation was composed of the upper income brackets. A survey the following month in *France Soir* produced similar French results.

15   Elliot J. Feldman and Jerome Milch, *Technocracy verus Democracy: The Comparative Politics of International Airports* (Boston: Auburn House, 1982), pp. 81, 91.

16   *Flight International*, July 17, 1976, p. 123.

17   Milton S. Hochmuth, *Organizing the Transnational: The Experience with Transnational Enterprise in Advanced Technology* (Leiden: A. W. Sijthoff, 1974), p. 135.

18   See ibid., p. 139, for an emphasis on these differences.

19   Ibid., p. 138.

20   Frank Melville, in *Fortune*, January 30, 1978.

21   *Economist*, March 23, 1974.

22   Elliot J. Feldman, "Patterns of Failure in Government Megaprojects: Economics, Politics and Participation in Industrial Democracies," in Samuel P. Huntington and Joseph Nye, eds., *Global Dilemmas: The World of the 1980s* (Cambridge, Mass., and Washington, D.C.: Harvard University Center for International Affairs and University Press of America, 1985).

23   Jean Steinberg, "Les problèmes posés par la realisation des villes nouvelles de la region d'Ile de France," 2 vols., doctoral diss., Université de Paris IV, 1978, pp. 339–78. My thanks to Luther Allen for calling this work to my attention.

24   For a more extended discussion, see Elliot J. Feldman, "An Antidote for Apology, Service and Witchcraft in Policy Analysis," in Phillip Gregg, ed., *Problems of Theory in Policy Analysis* (Lexington, Mass.: Lexington Books, 1976).

25   See, for example, criticisms of the public hearings in Cook, *The Stansted Affair*, p. 52.

26   Useful examples of the Italian argument include Vera Lutz, *Italy: A Study in Economic Development* (London: Oxford University Press, 1962); and M. V. Posner and S. J. Woolf, *Italian Public Enterprise* (London: Duckworth, 1967).

27   For a useful discussion comparing Britain with France, and contradicting stereotypes, see Jerry Webman, *Reviving the Industrial City: The Politics of Urban Renewal in Lyon and Birmingham* (New Brunswick, N.J.: Rutgers University Press, 1982).

MN THODOLOGICAL APPENDIX

1   Richard Schultz, *Federalism, Bureaucracy, and Public Policy* (Montreal: McGill-Queen's, 1980), p. 170.

2   Harry Eckstein, "Case Study and Theory in Political Science," in Fred Greenstein and Nelson Polsby, eds., *Handbook of Political Science* (Reading, Mass.: Addison-Wesley, 1975), VII, p. 138.

3   Arend Lijphart, "Comparative Politics and the Comparative Method," *American Political Science Review* 65 (September 1971), pp. 682–93.

4   Alexander George, "Case Studies and Theory Development: The Method of Structured, Focused Comparison," in Paul Gordon Lauren, ed., *Diplomacy: New Approaches in History, Theory, and Policy* (New York: Free Press, 1979), p. 60.

5   Robert T. Golembiewski, William A. Welsh, and William J. Crotty, *A Methodological Primer for Political Scientists* (Chicago: Rand McNally, 1969), p. 238.

6   Ibid., p. 236.

7   Roy Macridis and Bernard Brown, eds., *Comparative Politics: Notes and Readings* (Homewood, Ill.: Dorsey Press, 1955).

8   George, "Case Studies and Theory Development," p. 49.

9   Despite the pioneering comparison of Gabriel Almond and Sidney Verba, *The Civic Culture* (Princeton, N.J.: Princeton University Press, 1963), the series it spawned deploying a framework of structural-functionalism was published by Little Brown as single-country studies.

10   Terrence A. Tatje, "Problems of Concept Definition for Comparative Studies," in Raoul Narol and Ronald Cohen, eds., *Handbook of Method in Cultural Anthropology* (Garden City, N.Y.: Natural History Press, 1970), p. 689.

11   Robert C. Hunt, *The Comparative Method and the Study of Irrigation Social Organization*, Cornell Rural Sociology Bulletin Series (Ithaca, N.Y.: Cornell University Department of Rural Sociology, 1979), pp. 6, 7.

12   R. Bruce W. Anderson, "On the Comparability of Meaningful Stimuli in Cross-Cultural Research," *Sociometry* 30 (1976), p. 124.

13   Rodney Neeham, "Polythetic Classification: Convergence and Consequences," *Man*, n.s. 10 (1975), pp. 349–69.

14   Hunt, "The Comparative Method," p. 11.

15   Adam Przeworski and Henry Teune, *The Logic of Comparative Social Inquiry* (New York: Wiley, 1973). See also Henry Teune, "A Logic of Comparative Policy Analysis," in Douglas Ashford, ed., *Comparing Public Policies: New Concepts and Methods* (Beverly Hills, Calif.: Sage Yearbooks in Politics and Public Policy, 1978).

16   Lijphart, "Comparative Politics."

17   Robert K. Yin, "The Case Study Crisis: Some Answers," *Administrative Science Quarterly* 26 (March 1981), p. 63.

18   George, "Case Studies and Theory Development," p. 60.

19   Lijphart, "Comparative Politics," p. 687.

20   Sidney Verba, "Some Dilemmas in Comparative Research," *World Politics*, October 1967, pp. 111–27; see especially p. 118.

21   Christopher Leman, *The Collapse of Welfare Reform: Political Institutions, Policy and the Poor in Canada and the United States* (Cambridge, Mass.: MIT Press, 1980); Seymour Martin Lipset, *Political Man* (Garden City, N.Y.: Doubleday, Anchor Books, 1963); Seymour Martin Lipset, *Revolution and Counterrevolution* (Garden City, N.Y.: Doubleday, Anchor Books, 1970); Seymour Martin Lipset, "Radicalism in North America: A Comparative View of the Party Systems in Canada and the United States," *Transactions of the Royal Society of Canada*, ser. 4, vol. 14 (1976); Robert Presthus, guest ed., "Special Number on Cross-National Perspectives: United States and Canada," *International Journal of Comparative Sociology* 18, nos. 1–2 (March–June 1977).

22   George, "Case Studies and Theory Development," p. 52.

23   Hunt, "The Comparative Method," pp. 36–7.

24   Lijphart, "Comparative Politics," p. 692.

25   Joseph LaPalombara, "Macrotheories and Microapplications in Comparative Politics," *Comparative Politics* 1 (October 1968), pp. 60–77.

26   Hugh Stretton, *The Political Sciences: General Principles of Selection in Social Science and History* (London: Routledge & Kegan Paul, 1969), pp. 159–60.

Select bibliography

FRENCH AND BRITISH POLITICS AND POLICY

Ashford, Douglas. "Are Britain and France 'Unitary'?" *Comparative Politics* 9 (July 1977), pp. 483–99.

English Centralism and French Pragmatism: Central–Local Policymaking in the Welfare State. London: Allen & Unwin, 1982.

Beer, Samuel. *British Politics in the Collectivist Age.* New York: Random House, Vintage Books, 1965.

Beer, Samuel, Suzanne Berger, Guido Goldman, and Adam Ulam. *Patterns of Government: The Major Political Systems of Europe.* New York: Random House, 1973.

Blondel, Jean. *Voters, Parties and Leaders: The Social Fabric of British Politics.* Harmondsworth: Penguin Books, 1963.

Burke, Edmund. *Reflections on the Revolution in France.* New York: Bobbs-Merrill for the Liberal Arts Press, 1955.

Butler, David, and Donald Stokes. *Political Change in Britain: The Evolution of Electoral Choice.* 2d ed. New York: St. Martin's Press, 1974.

Cain, Bruce E. "Challenges and Responses in British Party Politics." *Comparative Politics,* April 1980.

Commissariat Général du Plan. *Rapport de la Commission des Transports et Communications, Préparation du 7ᵉ Plan.* Paris: La Documentation Française, 1976.

Crewe, Ivor, Bo Sarlvik, and James Alt. "Partisan Dealignment in Britain, 1964–1974." *British Journal of Political Science,* April 1977.

Crosland, Susan. *Tony Crosland.* London: Jonathan Cape, 1982.

Crossman, R. H. S. *The Diaries of a Cabinet Minister.* Vol. II. London: Hamish Hamilton & Jonathan Cape, 1968.

Crozier, Michel. *The Bureaucratic Phenomenon.* Chicago: University of Chicago Press, 1964.

La société bloquée. Paris: Seuil, 1970.

Ehrmann, Henry. "Politics in France." In Gabriel Almond and G. Bingham Powell, Jr., eds., *Comparative Politics Today: A World View.* 2d ed. Boston: Little Brown, 1980.

Finer, S. E. *The Changing British Party System, 1945–1979.* Washington, D.C.: American Enterprise Institute, 1980.

Gilpin, Robert. *France in the Age of the Scientific State.* Princeton, N.J.: Princeton University Press, 1968.

Gremion, Pierre. "La théorie de l'apprentissage institutionel." In Michel Crozier, ed., *Où va l'administration française?* Paris: Editions Organisations, 1974.

Hall, Peter A. "French Etatism versus British Pluralism." Manuscript, Harvard University Center for European Studies, July 1978.

Hewitt, Christopher. "Policy-Making in Postwar Britain: A Nation-Level Test of Elitist and Pluralist Hypotheses." *British Journal of Political Science* 4 (1974), pp. 187–216.

Kesselman, Mark. *The Ambiguous Consensus: A Study of Local Government in France.* New York: Knopf, 1967.

Machin, Howard. "Local Government Change in France – The Case of the 1964 Reforms." *Policy and Politics* 3, no. 2 (1974).

Massé, Pierre. "L'Europe et l'idée de programmation économique." *Révue du Marché Commun,* no. 55, February 1963.

Safran, William. *The French Polity.* New York: McKay, 1977.

Sarlvik, Bo, and Ivor Crewe. *The Conservative Victory of 1979.* Cambridge: Cambridge University Press, 1983.

Steinberg, Jean. "Les problèmes posés par la realisation des villes nouvelles de la region d'Ile de France." 2 vols. Doctoral diss., Université de Paris IV, 1978.

Webman, Jerry. *Reviving the Industrial City: The Politics of Urban Renewal in Lyon and Birmingham.* New Brunswick, N.J.: Rutgers University Press, 1982.

Wright, Vincent. *Government and Politics of France.* 2d ed. rev. London: Hutchinson, 1983.

COMPARATIVE PUBLIC POLICY

Cohen, Stephen. *Modern Capitalist Planning: The French Model.* Cambridge, Mass.: Harvard University Press, 1969.

Feldman, Elliot J. "An Antidote for Apology, Service and Witchcraft in Policy Analysis." In Phillip Gregg, ed., *Problems of Theory in Policy Analysis.* Lexington, Mass.: Lexington Books, 1976.

"Comparative Public Policy: Field or Method?" *Comparative Politics,* Winter 1978, pp. 287–305.

"Patterns of Failure in Government Megaprojects: Economics, Politics and Participation in Industrial Democracies." In Samuel P. Huntington and Joseph Nye, eds., *Global Dilemmas: The World of the 1980s.* Cambridge, Mass., and Washington, D.C.: Harvard University Center for International Affairs and University Press of America, 1985.

Hall, Peter, *Great Planning Disasters.* Berkeley: University of California Press, 1980.

Hayward, Jack. "Have British Planners Learnt from Experience?" *Government and Opposition,* Winter 1979.

"Institutional Inertia and Political Impetus in France and Britain." *European Journal of Political Research* 4 (1976), pp. 341–59.

"National Aptitudes for Planning in Britain, France and Italy." *Government and Opposition,* Autumn 1974.

"The Politics of Planning in France and Britain." *Comparative Politics,* January 1975.

Hayward, Jack, and Michael Watson, eds. *Planning, Politics and Public Policy: The British, French and Italian Experience.* Cambridge: Cambridge University Press, 1975.

Heidenheimer, Arnold J., Hugh Heclo, and Carolyn Teich Adams. *Comparative Public Policy: The Politics of Social Choice in Europe and America.* New York: St. Martin's Press, 1975.

Isaak, Robert A. *European Politics: Political Economy and Policy Making in Western Democracies.* New York: St. Martin's Press, 1980.

Lutz, Vera. *Central Planning for the Market Economy: An Analysis of the French Theory and Experience.* London: Longmans, 1969.

Italy: A Study in Economic Development. London: Oxford University Press, 1962.

McArthur, John, and Bruce Scott. *Industrial Planning in France.* Boston: Harvard Business School, 1969.

McLennan, Barbara N. *Comparative Politics and Public Policy.* North Scituate, Mass.: Duxbury Press, 1980.

Milch, Jerome E. "Paris Is Not France: Policy Outputs and Political Values in Two French Cities." Doctoral diss., MIT, 1973.

Peyrefitte, Alain. *Le mal français.* Paris: Librairie Plon, 1976.

Posner, M.V., and S. J. Woolf. *Italian Public Enterprise.* London: Duckworth, 1967.

Shonfield, Andrew. *Modern Capitalism: The Changing Balance of Public and Private Power.* Oxford: Oxford University Press, 1965.

Suleiman, Ezra. *Politics, Power and Bureaucracy in France: The Administrative Elite.* Princeton, N.J.: Princeton University Press, 1974.

Thoenig, Jean-Claude. *L'ere des technocrates.* Paris: Editions Organisations, 1973.

Vogel, David. "Coercion versus Consultation: A Comparison of Environmental Protection Policy in the United States and Great Britain." Paper presented at the APSA Annual Convention, Denver, Colo., September 1982.

COMPARATIVE POLITICS

Almond, Gabriel, and G. Bingham Powell, Jr., eds. *Comparative Politics Today: A World View.* 2d ed. Boston: Little, Brown, 1980.

Almond, Gabriel, and Sidney Verba. *The Civic Culture.* Princeton, N.J.: Princeton University Press, 1963.

Anderson, R. Bruce W. "On the Comparability of Meaningful Stimuli in Cross-Cultural Research." *Sociometry* 30 (1976).

Ashford, Douglas, ed. *Comparing Public Policies: New Concepts and Methods.* Beverly Hills, Calif.: Sage Yearbooks in Politics and Public Policy, 1978.

Eckstein, Harry. "Case Study and Theory in Political Science." In Fred Greenstein and Nelson Polsby, eds., *Handbook of Political Science.* Reading, Mass.: Addison-Wesley, 1975.

George, Alexander. "Case Studies and Theory Development: The Method of Structured, Focused Comparison." In Paul Gordon Lauren, ed., *Diplomacy: New Approaches in History, Theory, and Policy.* New York: Free Press, 1979.

George, Alexander, and Richard Smoke. *Deterrence in American Foreign Policy: Theory and Practice.* New York: Columbia University Press, 1974.

Golembiewski, Robert T., William A. Welsh, and William J. Crotty. *A Methodological Primer for Political Scientists.* Chicago: Rand McNally, 1969.

Hunt, Robert C. *The Comparative Method and the Study of Irrigation Social Organization.* Cornell Rural Sociology Bulletin Series. Ithaca, N.Y.: Cornell University Department of Rural Sociology, 1979.

LaPalombara, Joseph. "Macrotheories and Microapplications in Comparative Politics." *Comparative Politics* 1 (October 1968), pp. 60–77.

Leman, Christopher. *The Collapse of Welfare Reform: Political Institutions, Policy, and the Poor in Canada and the United States.* Cambridge, Mass.: MIT Press, 1980.

Lijphart, Arend. "Comparative Politics and the Comparative Method." *American Political Science Review* 65 (September 1971), pp. 682–93.

Lipset, Seymour Martin. *Political Man.* Garden City, N.Y.: Doubleday, Anchor Books, 1963.

——— "Radicalism in North America: A Comparative View of the Party Systems in Canada and the United States." *Transactions of the Royal Society of Canada,* ser. 4, vol. 14 (1976).

——— *Revolution and Counterrevolution.* Garden City, N.Y.: Doubleday, Anchor Books, 1970.

Lowi, Theodore J. *The End of Liberalism.* New York: Norton, 1969.

McConnell, Grant. *Private Power and American Democracy.* New York: Knopf, 1966.

Macridis, Roy, and Bernard Brown, eds. *Comparative Politics: Notes and Readings.* Homewood, Ill.: Dorsey Press, 1955.

Needham, Rodney. "Polythetic Classification: Convergence and Consequences." *Man*, n.s. 10 (1975), pp. 349–69.

Neustadt, Richard E. *Alliance Politics.* New York: Columbia University Press, 1970.

Presthus, Robert, guest ed. "Special Number on Cross-National Perspectives: United States and Canada." *International Journal of Comparative Sociology* 18, nos. 1–2 (March–June 1977).

Przeworski, Adam, and Henry Teune. *The Logic of Comparative Social Inquiry.* New York: Wiley, 1973.

Putnam, Robert. *The Beliefs of Politicians: Ideology, Conflict, and Democracy in Britain and Italy.* New Haven, Conn.: Yale University Press, 1973.

Schultz, Richard. *Federalism, Bureaucracy, and Public Policy.* Montreal: McGill-Queen's, 1980.

Smelser, Neil J. "The Methodology of Comparative Analysis." In D. P. Warwick and S. Osherson, eds., *Comparative Research Methods.* Englewood Cliffs, N.J.: Prentice-Hall, 1973.

"Notes on the Methodology of Comparative Analysis of Economic Activity." In *Transactions of the Sixth World Congress of Sociology.* Evian, France: International Sociological Association, 1966.

Stretton, Hugh. *The Political Sciences: General Principles of Selection in Social Science and History.* London: Routledge & Kegan Paul, 1969.

Tatje, Terrence A. "Problems of Concept Definition for Comparative Studies." In Raoul Narol and Ronald Cohen, eds., *Handbook of Method in Cultural Anthropology.* Garden City, N.Y.: Natural History Press, 1970.

Verba, Sidney. "Some Dilemmas in Comparative Research." *World Politics,* October 1967, pp. 111–27.

Yin, Robert K. "The Case Study Crisis: Some Answers." *Administrative Science Quarterly* 26 (March 1981).

CIVIL AVIATION

Adams, John G. U. "London's Third Airport, from TLA to Airstrip One." *Geographical Journal,* 1971, pp. 468–93.

Aéroports Magazine, no. 61, April 1976, published by Aéroport de Paris.

Ailleret, F. "L'exploitation des aérogares, passagers, et de fret à Roissy." In *Roissy en France.* Paris: Aéroport de Paris, 1973.

Airport Strategy for Great Britain. Department of Trade. London: HMSO, 1976.

Airports Authority Act, Elizabeth II, 1965.

Assembly of Western European Nations. *Guidelines for an Aviation Policy for Europe: Report.* Strasbourg, 1973.

Association of European Airlines. *Airport Study.* Brussels, 1976.

Bendixson, Terence. "Cublington Crash Landing." *New Statesman*, December 25, 1970.

British Airports Authority. *Report and Accounts 1965–66, 1966–67, 1967–68, 1968–69, 1969–70, 1970–71, 1971–72, 1972–73, 1973–74.*

British Airways. "Concorde Appraisal." Mimeographed, London, 1974.

Bromhead, Peter. *The Great White Elephant of Maplin Sands.* London: Paul Eletz, 1973.

Clark, F. G., and Arthur Gibson. *Concorde: The Story of the World's Most Advanced Passenger Aircraft.* London: Phoebus Publishing, 1976.

Closets, François de. *La France et ses mensonges.* Paris: Denoël/Gonthier, 1978.

Cmnd. 1916. *Agreement between the Government of the United Kingdom of Great Britain and Northern Ireland and the Government of the French Republic regarding the Development and Production of a Civil Supersonic Transport Aircraft.* London: HMSO, 1962.

Cmnd. 7084. *Airports Policy.* London: HMSO, 1978.

Commission on the Third London Airport. *Report.* London: HMSO, 1971.

Committee of Inquiry into Civil Air Transport. *British Air Transport in the Seventies.* London: HMSO, 1969.

Cook, Olive. *The Stansted Affair: A Case for the People.* London: Pan Books, 1967.

Costello, John, and Terry Hughes. *Concorde Conspiracy.* New York: Scribner's, 1976.

Davis, John. *The Concorde Affair.* London: Frewin, 1969.

Delepiere-Nys, Christiane, for Air Europe. *La politique de coopération entre les Compagnies Aériennes de l'Europe des six.* Brussels: Editions de l'Université de Bruxelles, 1974.

Dreyfus, Gilbert. "Il fallait construire l'aéroport de Roissy-en-France." In *Roissy en France.* Paris: Aéroport de Paris, 1973.

Fallot, Evelyne. "Un Facteur Nommé Concorde." *L'Express*, August 14, 1981.

Feldman, Elliot J., and Jerome Milch. "Options on the Metropolitan Fringe: Strategies of Airport Development." In Douglas Ashford, ed., *National Resources and Urban Policy.* New York: Methuen, 1980.

The Politics of Canadian Airport Development: Lessons for Federalism. Durham, N.C.: Duke University Press, 1983.

Technocracy versus Democracy: The Comparative Politics of International Airports. Boston: Auburn House, 1982.

Fifth Report from the Estimates Committee: London's Airports. Session 1960–1, HCP 233. London: HMSO.

Forestier, Jean. "Concorde: Le pari du vieux continent." *AviMag 672* (December 15, 1975).

Foster, Christopher, J. B. Heath, G. H. Peters, J. E. Ffowcs Williams, and Sir Peter Masefield. *Lessons of Maplin: Is the Machinery for Governmental Decision-Making at Fault?* London: Institute of Economic Affairs, 1974.

Gonzales, Arturo. "Making Concorde Flying Medically Safe." *Point International,* June 2, 1978.

Hall, Peter. "Roskill's Felicitous Calculus." *New Society,* February 19, 1970.

Henderson, David. "Two British Errors: Their Probable Size and Some Possible Lessons." *Oxford Economic Papers* 29 (July 1977).

Hochmuth, Milton S. *Organizing the Transnational: The Experience with Transnational Enterprise in Advanced Technology.* Leiden: A. W. Sijthoff, 1974.

Horwitch, Mel. *Clipped Wings: The American SST Conflict.* Cambridge, Mass.: MIT Press, 1982.

Hurren, B. J. *Britain and World Air Transport.* London: John Crowther, 1943.

Knight, Geoffrey. *Concorde: The Inside Story.* London: Weidenfeld & Nicolson, 1976.

McCrindle, R. A., and P. Godfrey. *Investigation into Rolls Royce.* London: HMSO, 1973.

McKie, David. "Buried in the Sands," *Guardian,* March 13, 1974.

A Sadly Mismanaged Affair: A Political History of the Third London Airport. London: Croom Helm, 1973.

Maplin: Review of Airport Project. London: HMSO, 1974.

May, Annabelle. "Concorde – Bird of Harmony or Political Albatross: An Examination in the Context of British Foreign Policy." *International Organization* 33 (Autumn 1979), pp. 481–508.

Ministry of Aviation. *Report of the Inter-Departmental Committee on the Third London Airport.* CAP 199. London: HMSO, 1964.

Ministry of Housing and Local Government. *Report of the Inquiry into Local Objections to the Proposed Development of Land at Stansted as the Third London Airport.* London: HMSO, 1967.

Mishan, E. J. "What Is Wrong with Roskill?" *Journal of Transport Economics and Policy,* September 1970.

de Neufville, Richard. *Airport Systems Planning.* Cambridge, Mass.: MIT Press, 1976.

Nivet, Raymond. "An Airline's Approach to Aircraft Selection." Speech delivered to the Royal Aeronautical Society, Dublin Branch, January 17, 1977.

Nwanery, V. C. "Equity in Cost–Benefit Analysis: A Case Study of the Third London Airport." *Journal of Transport Economics and Policy,* September 1970.

Organisme Régional d'Etudes Pour l'Aménagement de la Picardie. *Le Sud de la Picardie et l'Aéroport Charles de Gaulle.* Amiens: OREAP, 1974.

Owen, Kenneth. *Concorde: New Shape in the Sky.* London: Science Books International. 1982.

Paul, M. E. "Can Aircraft Noise Nuisance Be Measured in Money?" *Oxford Economic Papers,* November 1971.

Perman, David. *Cublington: A Blueprint for Resistance.* London: Bodley Head, 1973.

"Pourquoi un Troisième aéroport Parisien à Roissy?" *Bulletin OACI,* January 1983, pp. 19–20.

Powell, Clemans A. *Judgement of Relative Noisiness of a Supersonic Transport and Several Commercial Service Aircrafts.* Washington, D.C.: NASA, 1977.

Report of the London Airport Development Committee. CAP 145. London: HMSO, 1957.

Rordham, P.C. "Airport Planning in the Context of the Third London Airport." *Economic Journal* 80 (June 1970).

Scott, Robert J. "The Jetport Location Dilemma: Politics, Parochialism, and the Public Interest." Master's thesis, Cornell University, 1973.

Sealy, Kenneth R. *Airport Strategy and Planning.* Oxford: Oxford University Press, 1976.

Self, Peter. "Cost–Benefit Analysis and the Roskill Commission." *Political Quarterly* 41, no. 3 (1970).

Wiggs, Richard. *Concorde: The Case Against Supersonic Transport.* London: Ballantine for Friends of the Earth, 1971.

Wilson, Andrew. *The Concorde Fiasco.* Harmondsworth: Penguin Books, 1973.

(Also useful have been various issues of Aviation Week and Space Technology, Economist, L'Express, Le Figaro, Flight International, Fortune, France Soir, Guardian, Hansard's, L'Humanité, London Observer, Le Monde, New Society, New Statesman, New York Times, Le Point, *and* Times *[London]).*

Index